I0453383

THE TRUTH ON WATER

THE TRUTH ON WATER

A Collection of True Stories of One Woman's Risk, Discovery, and Survival

BOBBI RATHERT

Hey There, Hannah

Copyright @ 2023 Bobbi Rathert

Publishing Coordinator
Hannah Amann · Hey There, Hannah

Indie Editorial Service
Ashley Walsh

First Printing, October 2023
Printed in the United States of America

All Rights Reserved
No part of this book may be used or reproduced in any manner
whatsoever, stored in a retrieval system, or transmitted in any form
or by any means (electronic, mechanical, photocopy, recording,
scanning, or other) without the prior written permission from the
author or agents thereof.

ISBN-13: 979-8-218-29956-9

Cover Illustration
Illustration · Watercolor @ Bobbi Rathert 2023

The stories in this book reflect the author's reminiscence of experiences. Specific names, locations, and identifying characteristics may have been altered to protect the privacy of persons and places depicted. Dialogue, descriptions, impressions, and geographical aspects have been recreated from memory.

For my mom, my child,
my friend, my sister,
and my dog

CONTENTS

FOR THESE REASONS

Preface

This book is a collection of stories that rose during my time on the river, in my night camps, on river banks and islands, and in my mind, as I crossed six hundred and fifty miles of wild and beautiful river.

I am a sixty-nine-year-old woman who wanted to kayak the Mississippi River. Alone.

I have always had a secret affair with curiosity, which sparked my idea to go. It has influenced my decisions, travels, and lifelong work with people. Insight about anything else comes from the depths of this love story. The world is enormous, so I have gone out to see it. The Mississippi River was no different, so in 2022, I went.

To add fulfillment and community, I wanted my kayak journey to raise awareness for unity and equity in my hometown of La Crosse, Wisconsin. This is why *Paddling for Hope* was created by a like-minded team of organizers and planners to encourage harmony and diversity in our city. The initiative spread across the U.S. and into eleven distant countries.

Support and interest continue on our social media and website: *Paddling for Hope Facebook* and *paddlingforhope.com*.

It is gratifying to share these stories with you.

COLORFUL WASH ON A RIVER

Prologue

I love color. I am invariably drawn to gravity's natural and fluid pull on watercolor when brushed across cold-press fibers. The paper has a terrain of creases and chines that grab the paint or let it run freely. Forgivable paper and a merciful, colorful wash. The pigment spills and pools. It has a desire and cannot be controlled or predicted as willingly as oil paint on canvas or acrylic applied to its board. A lot like a boat on water, color goes where it must.

Working a watercolor and observing the completed image provokes a feeling of what comes off the river surface. Metamorphic texture, color, and spirit. The watercolor pans look like candy, each with its own taste, good enough to bite. Incomparable. I love their aesthetic beauty. But the river colors are wild and more dangerous, yet still beautiful.

The illustration on the book cover is a watercolor I finished a year after my river trip. I wanted it to epitomize the layered profusion of emotion that pours off the river when a person is living out there. Especially alone. Feelings blend while others come solo. Moody. Curious, tender, and longing. Spiritual, maybe peaceful, or then afraid. Sentimental. Mighty, happy, meditative, and weak. Fatigue and energy took turns. At times, a haunting power rose, or a barren and gloomy essence could not be escaped. On the same day, optimism and confidence were like air, so plentiful that I could breathe it in. But thirst was a constant.

The banner image seen on the Paddling for Hope website *(paddlingforhope.com)* represented my river trip and was used for the *Paddling for Hope* initiative. It is a small portion of a larger watercolor I completed a few years earlier. The original image is a diverse crowd gathered for a shared purpose and with the same hope that change will come.

My anticipation and hopefulness on the river
that came from this image were profound.

THE SIX HUNDRED FIFTY CHAPTERS

Introduction

While planning and announcing my kayak trip on the Mississippi River, I was frequently asked if I was going to the Gulf of Mexico. My answer was *it is my hope*, or *that is my plan*. I wanted to do all the miles but was unsure how it would unfold. I knew about paddling and camping, each separately. But it was new for me to pair them up over weeks alone, loaded with gear and provisions, on a big river. There was no way to foretell what might happen.

A few other midlife and older women had solo-paddled before me, but not many. It was a daring and phenomenal adventure, and at sixty-eight, I felt its unconventional nature was directly upon me.

Like most high-hope paddlers, I wanted to complete twenty-four hundred miles of the river, from the headwaters to the gulf. Many people have done it, some in sections over time, others in one long and linear summer. But more have not gone the entire length despite much optimism. I was one of these. Paddlers who end sooner than hoped have good reasons. I have heard several of them, and I had my own.

Many people who followed my river trip read my blogs on the *Paddling for Hope* website and social media. These writings are about my river progress, reflections, and events as they took place. I wrote them every few days, usually when settled in camp or inside my tent before a night's sleep. For this book, I have expanded the blogs with added stories from the river and other adventures of my life.

In this book's end chapters, I have written about why my trip stopped - suddenly, regrettably, and short of my goal. These chapters are *Almost*, *Belong*, and *Water*.

To inform followers that I had returned home, I posted a blog entitled *Six Hundred Fifty* that separated my six hundred fifty mile journey into essential sections that, for me and I hoped for them, brought a culminating perspective to my time on the river. The blog's nine subjects were developed further and became eight short stories in this book's *Six Hundred Fifty* segment.

But first, let's start at the beginning.

CHAPTER 1

The Unknowledge of Humans

It was a sunny and warm day when spring was late in coming. I looked out the window that morning and saw people walking, some without jackets or already in shorts and flimsy tops. I did not dress lightly but thought of pitching my tent to sleep outside that night. Some lighthearted simpleness was in order after deep winter when a long-anticipated bright day showed itself.

I had last written about my upcoming river trip when it was one hundred and eleven days out. I felt the jimjams when the numbered chart was now marked twenty-nine days. The Mississippi was in the news on river sites because other paddlers and I wanted to know water conditions and when we could go. It reminded me of over-exuberant town kids at first spring streaking back and forth on their bikes fresh out of basement storage, swooshing through puddles of snowmelt with high spirit, icy water sopping their clothes. Our mom would not allow it. *It will only snow again, and who will put all those bikes away then?* So boisterous with spring fever, we did not care about snow. And how did she even know it was coming again anyway?

News from the headwaters was wavering and caused me to mope a smidge like a kid without a bike in springtime. Too much water was risky, a gushing surge, but low water made pulling a boat on the stone river bottom hopelessly monotonous. These uncertain reports should have considered my sensible winterlong planning for a river trip in which I included only perfect water and no bears. I had not weighed in the thickness of two-foot ice left on the lakes or cold nights below the tolerance on my sleeping bag label. But I did prepare for enormous mosquitos and near-giant spiders, for which I had packed head nets and a far-reaching flyswatter.

Generally, I do not easily adapt to altered or unclear plans because readjusting is unsettling and can be a melodramatic challenge. Besides, humans are created to accept change only after being consulted. High water, late winter melt, and continued cold in the north upended my preconceived notion of how it would all go. It was unnerving.

*   *   *

I found comfort in the predictable behaviors of birds when I began studying them when I was young. After my mother died, I inherited her bird books and scope. Late one season, I was paddling along tree-lined banks of a large marsh to stay cool in its shade when I saw a handsome bird above me. It was smooth as velvet and brushed in matte color to accentuate its perfect outline. If I were a color namer, I'd have named this bird Chamois. Its surface was smooth and creamy. It was nothing like a river surface that was coarse and unthinking. The tip of its tail appeared to be dipped in vivid yellow butter, and its wing tips were dunked in bloody red. The bird wore a raccoon-like mask painted in the deepest smooth black like a posh bandit. If this finesse was not enough, it looked like it had combed its hair back into a sharply crested ducktail. That day, I could not stop looking at this creature made from a mystery.

What happened next was unexpected, nearly unbelievable. There suddenly were two, then four identical ones. They were gregarious, showing off like a classroom of eighth graders and moving from one branch to the next in quickened, excited energy. By the end, there were ten of these elegant, velvety birds, all the same, each one extroverted and following the others like a gang of nomads. I loved them right away and worried I would never see them again. But since that day, I have seen them from time to time, and most recently in my front yard, getting drunk on winter crabapples. They always behave the same and eat only fruits or berries without much deviation. They are more predictable than humans and never cause heartbreak like we do.

Even stinkhorns give this same satisfaction and are so habitual that they draw flies the same year after year, and their cherry-red, slimy stems never smell sweet and smooth but always like death. When stinkhorns first emerge, we are assured of their rapid growth, so quick we can see them move. They are never changing. People love the expectedness, even with its consistent gory stench. An ungovernable river holds no comparison against steadiness, this source of our equilibrium, but I still wouldn't trade the unruly downbound water for a stinkhorn. Humans are definitely drawn to certainty, but I continued to choose my paddle trip down a volatile river.

*   *   *

It is soul-rattling when we cannot look around corners, into the future, or even through night darkness. We revere fictional characters with magical powers and x-ray vision, and favor well-lit areas over shadowy stretches. Longing to see whatever we want, we cannot, despite the strength of our desire, and our predictive abilities are almost always below average. I packed maps, GPS, satellite, smartphone, and access to other paddlers' tales. Still, my uneasy relationship with uncertainty was detectable.

An overhead view of the first hundred miles of the Mississippi River shows how it snakes, switching back in curling form, which it does for countless miles. Stretches of the Mississippi in the south, below Baton Rouge, wind tightly along the way the same. Paddlers worry how to see around these river turns. How fast can a kayak go in reverse if a bear and her cubs are in the water just around a bend? A kayaker could come head-on with anything. I speculated about this at night while trying to sleep, and I dreamed of a gift my uncle gave me in 1966 when I was eleven.

It was a periscope with tiny mirrors inside and one end that swiveled. I put it to frequent and practical use. I could not believe this device belonged to me or operated as it did, and I wondered how my uncle knew it was an ideal gift for me, a sixth grader. I began to use it for everything, spying on birds and my sisters, pretending about things as if I were in the army or on a TV show. I hid under a pile of dried leaves, peering at people walking by. It was what all humans wanted, to see where our eyes can't see and remain clandestine while doing it. And now, an adult planning a long river trip, I wish I knew where my periscope was.

I paddled slowly in spring as a speeding motorboat came nearly airborne around a cusp and pointed directly at me, obviously both of us unable to see around the embankment. We were both startled and concerned. The driver was speeding, and I had drifted from the bank. He did not know what to do, so he swerved back and forth in a gamble about which way I would go. I did the same, shifting left to right, wondering what he would decide. We barely missed a direct impact, but I took on his considerable wake. After that, we both went our ways without looking back, pretending nothing happened. But here I am, telling of it still while writing about my river trip and our inability to know what is coming. It was just a near-death moment caused by the human inability to have future knowledge. We think we know or hope to know, or at least minimize what could happen because we do not know. What could be coming next in our own unknowing?

I had been thinking about the unknown as I counted down the last days and what would become of me. I knew some people who used drones to go on ahead and check for bears that might be headed toward camp or to spot a subdivision of new homes just beyond the treeline of their remote wilderness camp. The advantage was knowing the future and how many beaver dams blocked the way downstream or a gone-aground boat was planted in the bottom, concealed under years of climbing weeds and nesting birds, giving off a spooky air. But no one can know what they do not know, which means trouble for humans. We want to know about tomorrow when it is still today. We want to know what we will face before getting a good look at what we are already facing. I felt it as I packed my gear, putting in too much just in case or not enough. While packing and figuring out my travels, I repeatedly confessed that I did not know, but this did not help my confidence or the packing.

Human insight is frail and cannot be compared to the unknowable energy that makes molecules spin and vibrate. People are not that big. Are we really supposed to manipulate substance and matter? It makes us undependable when we declare what we only think is the truth. We would be stung less by admitting our unknowing than just pretending with smug overconfidence.

I tried to let go of the worry about a sizeable critter outside my tent, ready to gnaw, or a coiled snake poised to strike beneath my bed. I attempted to stop considering where I had yet to arrive and just tried to stay where I was. Whatever was around the next corner or behind where I could not see, whoever might want something I did not have, or what I must carry that is too heavy, the worry of it was more significant than the thing itself, so I tried to leave it alone. We cannot be left to our feeble ideas, finicky solutions, or what might threaten us in the dark.

People are not super enlightened or filled with their own wisdom but have only sparse knowledge, even at our peak competence. Humans are unreliable in this way because we think more highly of ourselves than we are. However many solutions we conceive, we must always resolve them again later.

As long as we have life, we ought to live it the only way we know and make the most of what faces us, using conscience as a compass. That is about it for the human condition. It is futile to brood over what plans might change or who opposes our stubborn will. This was my trouble as I planned to kayak the river. Should I stay or go, be safe or die? Was this a sound idea or ridiculous? I wondered *why am I going?* I felt unable to know. A person cannot discern a wolf in the flock, even if it is one of their own. We want to know everything beforehand but are unable, and then we don't even listen. I felt so foible that I hoped someone would stop me from going.

So the day came that I had to leave home with my boat on the car, gear loaded in back, and traveling with only sparse foresight. I went nearly four hundred miles with family and friends to our northern Minnesota lodging, wondering the entire way, *do I know enough?* As we drove, I watched the Mississippi River move. It appeared smarter than me, swift and bulging each time we crossed it.

Even though it narrowed progressively, it hoarded energy and its girth in an undetectable way. I knew it was cunning and planning against those who got on it, including me. I saw its mean streak as it rushed south, and I raced north to ride it back down. I thought, *why am I doing this?* Still, launch time crept closer every second. I had set this time for early the following day, but I wanted to cancel as if someone else had forced this on me.

It is natural to resist what we love, to want to give in to fear and discomfort, and stay home. But I continued toward it as time pushed me against gravity. Before dawn, I would pray, eat a meal, and go. Curiosity kills cats, but so far, it has not killed me.

I read a poem the day before I launched my boat on this secretive river. After our half-century friendship, my dear friend Lin gave it to me for my river travels. It was C. P. Cavafy's *Ithaka,* about the journey through life, filled with expectation and hopefulness, going out, rising well, and then returning loaded with treasure.

When my river trip was imminent, I was filled with surging emotions at all times those days and nights. I constantly speculated about paddling in solitude for hours and days and then sleeping alone in the night. I wondered, *would I long for human companionship and then, after the humans, ache for familiar solitude?* However it would go, I hoped to survive it and return home carrying all kinds of jewels stuffed in the hatches and weighting my overfilled mind.

My friend Christi said *you'll write a book.* But I would say, *maybe. I just don't know.* Some of my stories are treasures from my encounters with *Ithaka* and whether I prevailed over the many moments of truth. Others are from different times that I survived, but just barely.

I have been home for ten months, remembering what it was like to prepare, writing in hindsight about the river, its uncertainty, confidence, my betraying weakness, inhaling, swelling, rising, and coming home. This is my faithful life where only love breaks up trouble. It is comforting to be home, writing and thinking only in memories.

CHAPTER 2

Anne Street

I was five years old when I stood on Anne Street staring above at two concrete sculptures that seemed taller than an old sugar pine. Perhaps I was just thirty-six inches tall but by only a hair's width. We were on a road trip to Canada, my mom, her mom, my two siblings, and me after my dad was killed and other tragic things happened. All this caused my maternal grandma to set off on this long and distant journey with us loaded in the back of a 1957 Bel Air Nomad, the first big purchase for my mother alone.

Its front end was like a Corvette with a station wagon rear, covered in hard polished chrome and two-tone blue with white. My mom bought it after she abruptly and only recently was widowed at twenty-nine with three tender-age children and no prospects for income. My grandmother intended to get us out of town and onto a straighter path, away from the grief that filled our house and skewed my mother's ability to think without doubting. We had barely fledged when my dad was buried on his thirtieth birthday, so a road trip made perfect sense to these two women, now heads of our household. What better way to feel safe after heartbreak than to bundle loved ones into a tight little space?

Whether my grandma drove us toward restoration or only away from the unraveling was a mystery. Still, things were no different when we returned home weeks later. Ultimately, my family would not recover from its grave injury, leaving us all scattered.

*　　*　　*

Years passed, decades even, when I found myself on Anne Street again facing the tall statues, Paul Bunyan with Babe the Blue Ox, for the second time in my life. Constructed in 1937 for one original purpose – attracting travelers to Bemidji - they have accomplished that in far-off northern Minnesota ever since. Because of their appeal, they became American icons like Wall Drug's eighty-foot dinosaur and the giant ball of twine in Kansas. Almost a century since the Anne Street characters were delivered into town parade-style, with Babe set on a fuel truck that sent exhaust through his nostrils.

In May 2022, I was there for an overnight before casting my gear-heavy kayak into the river's headwaters to move downstream on a well-intentioned paddle trip. In the morning, I left my lodging for my launch point below Winnibigoshish Dam and visited these landmarks with friends. Later a photograph revealed that my friend Pam had dressed the same as Paul but only by chance. She was not as tall and stood beside his leg, but both wore red plaid shirts, blue pants, and red socks. A correlation as believable as a fortune cookie, affirming not much more than simple harmony and freedom to be there a second time in life, and this time with friends, my travel-ready boat, and me sixty-three years older than before.

I felt it as we drove away from the statues toward the river. The reminiscence and familiar ache. It was nice to be there again, but later, I thought about it in silence as I went slowly downstream after launching and watched for dormant pieces of myself. Despite the possibilities on this long kayak journey, no matter my distance, I was fully aware that the only certainty with me was my unknowing. It was still just me over these significant miles ahead, and even just the few miles paddled since setting off, my back to my waving friends. As I floated away, I felt my dominion waning with each blade pull, and I could not help but wonder what awaited me on this river. As I sculled downstream that first morning, I began to feel relief from an unexpected calmness and a love for the water's smooth downward current. Both were confirmed only by things of the natural world surrounding me. For the first time in months, my river trip was not just a thought but actual and legitimate.

I wanted assurance of mercy for the days and weeks coming, but that only emanates from providence and a person's reliance on it. Humans are known to hesitate in their dependency when attempting to otherwise control. They strategize to secure their own needs and occasionally get only temporary and fallible outcomes.

Never are human efforts as sure as the midnight stars over my old barn where I stood thousands of nights, feet in the grass while seeing the southern sky outwards at fourteen hundred light-years beyond my tiny spot on the earth. Inside the constellation under Orion's belt is his sword smack in the nebula's heart. This is where, on good nights with a scope, a human eye might see blue-green harlequin swirls where baby stars incubate and more colors spin beyond our ability to see.

The star cluster is like watercolor on a brush, too full of fluid. It streams out and floods a space on the paper that gyres and spills into a nearby painted shape. The colors of both are different from what I intended, but they might be even better, or not. This is Orion's nebula wonder seen all over the earth wherever we stand, above us, and by no means fallible. Still, this is our assurance. Always in the night sky, whether above Cape Town or Nome, over Manila, or in Minnesota on the river, no matter where, it is always in place. I could go out right now, and it would be in the southern sky, sure and steady, even if blocked by layers of clouds. And not a super truth, but the truth. Itself enough.

*   *   *

My hope for assurance on the river reminded me of a red fox I followed with my truck along Three Chimney Road near my home farm. It swayed confidently on the gravel, in step with a large fluffy meal dangling side-to-side in its mouth like a quickened metronome. Whether feathers or fur, it was set on it for supper and food for its kits at the den, like any good parent. Its head pivoted my way, and its eyes glanced swiftly back out the corner to confirm it was trailed by a slow black truck, which was me. Then, the head spun forward again with dignity and poise. It did not move aside to give me room, nor did it run into the ditch with worry, but continued fully satisfied that this provision was theirs for the family back home. The fox had the elusive assurance that I wanted.

Humans want sureness of things just like this, not talking

about deservedness or entitlement, but a certainty that we will have food, some affection, a sense we are wanted, and a warm place to sleep at night. We hope to find the things we need right then, but it is more challenging than it sounds. Orion and a red fox are more confident and time-proved in trust than humans. In a blink of Orion's millions, Paul and Babe have stood in Bemidji, and foxes have found their meals. But I headed down the river with little assurance and this familiar feeling.

Despite the uncertainty, I did learn during those early days on my river trip that there were a few things I could depend upon. It began with my pant legs and feet always wet, if not soaking or at least just dampened. It was a given state of things. Mosquitoes were faithful also, showing up somewhere each day and always much more sizable than expected, about the scale of an aglet, and never late arriving or letting me down.

Along with them came ticks by the buckets full, and, as always, in each encounter, they refused to die no matter what I did. It was something I could depend on without any worry. One morning, I woke to a wood tick swimming the frog stroke in a drop of Deet repellent beside my pillow. Like mosquitoes, ticks overpower humans the same as punkies do. All these were very reliable and devoted to me, and I was never concerned they would be absent.

Known also as no-see-ums, punkies left red dots around my face and ears in a pattern only known to themselves as their secret. If I had wanted this pattern of red spots circling my scalp and the edge of my face, I would call up some punkies and never be disappointed. The punkie operator's manual might say that *punkies attack around the eyes, ears, scalp, and occasionally exposed arms and legs. Punkies, more petite than specks, crawl into sleeves, boots, or neckbands to penetrate other vulnerable places on the human, like their tender hearts where affection is stored, if a punkie could break through its crust.* But real-time punkies prefer the head just beneath the rim of a hat, laughing all the while they do it.

After a recent shower, I found two dog ticks taking free lunch from my leg. I yanked them out, then watched them swirl in the toilet bowl, whining like they didn't deserve it. These ticks don't die unless cut in half with the pinch of a fingernail, a try with my Leatherman, or a good drowning. Punkies do not die either because they are invisible, and mosquitoes don't seem to die, but that is just because they reproduce so quickly. We never know if they are those from yesterday or an entirely new bunch. Both mosquitos and punkies travel like ghosts through the air, very quiet, while ticks are clumsy and loud. They could not care less about a stealth reputation.

Deet turned out to be fickle. A random certainty, the wind as a breeze could keep punkies and mosquitos at home, but ticks came out anyway. Although I thought Deet would work for me, it did only sometimes. Mark that as unreliable.

*   *   *

One thing I took for granted and knew would never change was my inclination to keep to myself. Through the trip, there were many opportunities to interact with others, enjoy their company, and meet with local people. But after a greet-and-nod, a little visiting, and some small talk, I still found comfort when watching over myself.

One evening, a toothless, bearded man with an extra-large-eyed chihuahua in his bike basket rode into my camp near town. Sixties music blared from a speaker zip-tied to his electric bicycle. He asked if I wanted to visit with him, but he told his life story in a long, uninterrupted sentence. He did not wish to have a mutual conversation but to tell of himself instead. Afterward, he peddled off, singing louder than the speaker. That was Luke with his little dog, Duke. Although he was talkative, engaging, and curious, I wish I had been more skilled in yick-yacking whitter-whatter.

Three older adults strolled near my camp, then stopped. One asked, *are you the lady going to the gulf?* After I told them it was my hope, they stared at me in silence, mouths open, and then the man genuflected on my behalf before shuffling off. Our engagement did not lack all meaning because I knew I needed that blessing. The two ladies hesitated before following the man, and one looked at the other. *Is she going all the way in that skinny boat?* I never knew how they learned of my river plans.

Another man walked purposefully toward me, dangling a mini-mart sack that held an ice-cold quart of spring water. I almost buckled with delight when he reached out with it. *I thought you'd need this,* he said. Without hesitating, I swilled it after a day of warm water in muddy bottles rolling around my kayak bottom. This one was water-beaded, icy, and irresistible. He said he heard where I was camped, so he brought what I might need. We talked briefly, and then he gave me the weather report.

By now, an older man stood off, hesitant to interfere, but he eventually asked permission to approach. *My four-year-old grandson wants to see your boat,* he said. I was gentle with the boy, but he stayed behind his grandpa's leg, hitting the ground with a small stick. That was the extent of the interaction, as he felt more awkward than I did. I thought I would only engage a little with others, a certainty on my secluded river trip, but it was different from how it sometimes went. Strings of days went by with no people, not even a voice, but other days brought many my way.

I had no doubt I would remain strong in muscle, energy, spirit, and stamina throughout my entire trip and all the time. But this did not happen as anticipated. In many places, the Mississippi River flows through large bodies of water susceptible to changes and filled with secrets. On maps, the river's flow is marked in its natural direction as it goes on its own or through lakes that obscure it. These lakes have distinct currents, often separate from the speed and path of the river's course. Because the river's flow has its own style, the individuality of the Mississippi, it goes where it wants even when attempts to control it are everywhere.

When paddling through a large body, trouble comes because the river current is not drawn out in front or indicated with markers but only on digital or paper maps. This lack of definition or signage causes mistakes when paddling far one way when the river down under the lake goes another. One certainty is that it is not like an interstate or rural highway, evident with road signs and arrows or lights sometimes. The river, it's a mystery.

One day paddling, I abruptly opened into Blackwater Lake, a series of deep-water contours that sometimes had depths near seventy feet. Its water was predominantly black but translucent, with eight miles of wiggly shoreline all about five river miles northwest of the Pokegama Dam. In configurations of connected biological shapes pictured on my map, they appeared like an esophagus heading into a stomach that led to the pancreas. Then, swirling narrow intestines opened to vast bowels, with a gallbladder on the side to the south, itself a little fishing lake, but still connected.

The lake was teeming with black and brown bullhead, black crappie, yellow perch, walleye, pug nose, and pretty pumpkinseed with about a dozen other species of natural beauties. There were so many to choose from that no one with a pole was disappointed, and the many anglers in their boats that day proved it.

As for me, I thought I would never get to the end of this paddle, just like a swallowed peanut or supper plate of black turtle beans moving through the gauntlet of human digestion, with no way out but just through. The lake waves and blustery wind sounded like a baby's belly growl with other familiar gurgling noises, all overstimulating and distracting. Finding the river in this ruckus was challenging enough in the lake chain of organic shapes. But it was also bordered by large electric power plants that looked much like Oz, set back enough not to be scary but adequately close for intrigue.

As I went for hours and distance in thirteen mph headwinds, white caps were against me and overcoming my boat. I paddled with all my might but barely moved an inch forward sometimes. I hollered out, *make this wind stop!* But then added a more humbled, *please* because it was brutal and dehydrating, nearly blowing my face off, and I, by myself, could do nothing. Still, I could not stop paddling, even for a sip of water. If I did, I would have been driven back where I had been or into an unstoppable spin. I felt the test and knew I was failing. What took an hour on a quiet day was four hours or more on this very windy and loud morning.

I finally reached the Mississippi River outflow and thought I had moved into it left and north of the lake system. However, I mistakenly missed its turn due to poor navigation, no apparent markers, and the uproar of noise and commotion that made the distracting chaos. It was a real disappointment when I discovered that I had gone too far as if I needed a more exhausting encounter to prove something unknown. My mortal shortcomings were already in evidence to witnesses on the lakeshore, but no one came out to help. I continued paddling but in turn-around strokes to inch back to the river's calmer waters when, finally, its right turn rescued me from the wind's relentless updraft. It was pure relief when I arrived, where I could slow down and drift, rest my paddle, drink some water, and hang my head in exhaustion. There were five river miles yet to go this day.

I expected to be stronger after a ride like that, but it did not happen that way. At night in my tent, I read, *your weakness and strength are the same,* and I wondered, *who is this for?* But then I saw the wisdom, and it was for me. As I lowered my light and turned to sleep, I convinced myself that things on the river would go my way and according to plan tomorrow. This deception helped me drift into a sound sleep, deep as if I swallowed a sleeping pill.

It was early when I woke rested, wondering why I expected to meander on smooth water and chirp a melody throughout my river journey. I knew it was perilous out there, snakes and bears, all other biting creatures, river hidden in a lake, face-ripping gusts, unrelenting headwinds, falling trees, full-on exhaustion from oppositional currents, and I hadn't even reached the floods yet. The weather was alive like a human. I knew this but wished it wasn't true.

*   *   *

Two nights before, a storm was severe, sucking the air out and back into my tent with earth-rattling thunder. I braced on my back and felt its vibrations through the ground as it rolled beneath my camp like a burrowing animal. A passerby said, *tonight's storm will be worse with seventy-five mph surges.* He told me this as he glanced up at the trees, *I guess these might not fall on your tent,* he mumbled with little assurance. A River Angel, someone from an informal group of people who live along the river and offer assistance to paddlers, texted with urgency. *Take cover now!* he alarmed. *I'll drive two-and-a-half hours to get you!* Two others messaged for my location, each offering to pick me up, but I was on land already and knew they needed to rescue others still out there on the water.

For me, it was a calm and sunny day after a storm. So I missed the size of what was coming and had yet to make plans or notions of my own, alone here in this strange place. *Now what?* I wondered. Before I answered, I heard my voice speaking to a local taxi, wondering if they had a roof rack for my kayak. *No, sorry,* they said. I told them, *I must seek shelter, but am heavy with gear and a fifteen-foot boat.* Still, *no, but sorry,* I hung up, puzzling over my next move. I started breaking camp when my phone rang. It was the taxi. *Yes,* they said. I still don't know what changed their mind, but I felt thankful.

The first hotel I called accepted my boat to store in their

yurt, so I booked two nights' refuge. The taxi man and his dispatcher arrived at my camp in a rusty Bronco with a roof-top rack, loaded my belongings, fastened the boat, and drove me to my lodging. Minutes later, I was in my room with gear and my kayak, delivered and unloaded by the taxi man, who decided I should have my boat in the room, not the yurt.

That night, the thunder and lightning, solid howling winds, continuous sirens, and civil defense horns all sounded like a symphony of urgency. I was in a dry bed staring at light-ning flashes and red emergency lights strobe across the ceiling. Then I realized it. This is how it can sometimes go with humans. I could be in camp with gear flung in all directions, up tree limbs, and my boat smashed by a log. And me, afraid. I could be wrapped in the cold, wet nylon of my collapsed tent and clutching onto blades of grass to hold tight to Earth. But it was awesome where I was and how I got there. It was the humans checking, alerting, and delivering.

I dreamed I was in this room during the night, visualiz-ing the yurt cartwheeling across the parkway. My kayak was flipping inside, shoved over roads and into buildings by the storm's force. But really, my boat and I were safe inside after tornadoes touched down in towns along the river, and water rose over everything. I spent time reading, resting, meditat-ing, and sorting gear to lighten my load. A second taxi man took me to a shipping merchant who sent the extra weight back home.

Two days passed when the first taxi man returned to take me to the river. It was a sunny, cool morning after my hotel retreat, and I was grateful for its safe shelter. The brutal weather was over, but not before its devastation tore off roofs, downed trees, and flipped small buildings and vehicles. It left volumes of property damage, but no one was hurt, not even me. The river was smooth but swift that morning, rising from the stormwater at a nearby launch point. I hoped for a perfect day but considered how nothing is inevitable on a river.

As I packed my kayak on the riverbank, I heard noises above the boat ramp and along a row of young trees. I turned back to see what it was - taxis pulling in one by one. The dispatcher and drivers were waving. They had come to tell me goodbye. *Remarkable,* I thought while shaking my head in disbelief. I could only smile and wave back. These good people were there for me, so present when I needed humans the most, the angels and drivers the same. There I was, alive that morning, going downriver, needing nothing, and blessed.

*   *   *

A late spring melt upriver was causing enormous quantities of fast-moving water and high currents to rush down from the headwaters. The river was so ravaged that the DNR closed the first hundred miles. Various dams below were discharging wide open, making it only possible to portage and re-enter with help. The movement of water naturally quickened as it swelled and was breathtaking and frightening. I expected it to come at me from behind, but it was already waiting ahead.

When I settled on the river that perfect morning, I felt unified with the water as we moved south with the flow, drops held together by significant energy and heading toward the gulf to eventually cycle back again. Droplets of water and minutes collect on the river, passing inch by foot by mile, closer to my next night camp, then passing near home, and then to the oceans. For me, it all began on Anne Street then and again now.

CHAPTER 3

River Five Ways

Way of Calm Water. It was May when I put in at Winnie Dam, east of Lake Winnibigoshish, and had my first moments with this river water from the far north. It was smooth, clear, and shiny. *Agreeable,* I thought. I wanted this kind of water, and I got it, even though downriver dams were wide open. Assessing this water I was riding on was challenging, the same water spewing out of the barriers below and producing thunderous, frothy soup.

Its mood changed like a scary person who goes from calm and gentle to loud-mouthed and fitful at a spontaneous moment with no warning. Nobody wants to be around them. This unstable contrast set up my tentative relationship with the water these weeks I was on it.

On the first day, as I floated downriver, I sighed in relief that I was here after all the planning, and the water was good-natured. It was behaving one way, and that was how I liked it. After early morning launches, I enjoyed the first day and again the next, following my initial camp nights far from home and alone. It was always good and sound sleep, even though not enough. All had been going very well. That is what I often thought when each day's water was more perfect than the day before.

But I felt foolish, like when a new friend is made and trusted too soon, and they turn ugly before the beginning is over. On the river, there was no going back, even if this long thread of temperamental water controlled me with a whim. I had to remain steady and reliable the whole way down. So there I was, trusting and not trusting concurrently, which left me slightly nervous from being so exposed.

Way of Rising Water. There were other times when the river water showed this calmer side, like a human covertly controlling their brash tendencies and emotional lability. I often fell for that shameful trust but was nagged by the truth underneath. I knew there was more to it than this, but I enjoyed its good-hearted spirit so much that I kept the water's potential for change hidden in my blindside. I wrote about it later when I found myself in flood waters. I felt so betrayed. Of course, it felt like a trick I only assumed was planned for me. But then, I heard it happened to a fellow paddler the same.

I was paddling along, possibly humming a sing-songy tune inside my head, as the river cunningly swelled below my boat and started swirling quietly, filling every space of grazing land, woodlands, and hollows, without making a sound. It was disgusting how devious, but there was no time to think about it. At the same time, I circled the same sloppy, rapidly shifting, surging, deepening, whirling water paths that all ended in the identical location every time. I was rescued from the peril of that day by a sheriff's deputy on river patrol after I pressed my SOS signal button. But no one freed me from the skepticism that formed about the river, as if it was full of human potential.

Way of Deadly Water. In a different writing, I told how I nearly drowned in sudden circumstances and my own ignorance. River water always gets the upper hand, as if I had not known it before but needed a reminder. It gives no forewarning, and that's the point, like a parent who shouts, *do it now*! The element of surprise makes the river perilous as if delivered from the hand of something eviler than one could ever suspect. On this day, I missed the cues that, if I had noticed, go together into a complete picture of river character.

I was a guest on the water's estate and could not make any demands. The water changes its tempo, getting too full, not full enough, too fast, or not moving at all. This is the expressed will of water because it is at home there. If water came into my house through the roof or an open window, maybe a broken pipe, it is mine to speak about. But not there where I was, so far away from home on the day I almost drowned.

The river rose around me like a mean-hearted parent lurching across the table with a hard slap to the cheek. It came out of nowhere for an innocent slight and more hurtful to the heart than the face. The ugly feeling was not easily reversed, so this day left me with that slap sting and no faith in myself or my instincts. I was constantly surrounded by something meaner and more significant than me, or so I felt. It took days for it to wear off or maybe to never disappear, but I returned to the river anyway, glad I had not drowned completely. But I knew it was not entirely up to me that any of it happened the way it did.

Way of Sneaky Water. Lake Pepin was not a mistake but a necessity, like crossing a bridge with a troll underneath. It was notorious for blocking paddlers with its wind and waves. But I couldn't travel the rest of the river if I did not pass over it. The Coast Guard told me that unsuspecting paddlers are rescued throughout the summers. After hearing this and from my almost-drowning nearly two weeks before, I was not entirely confident. When I returned to paddling, the sting was still there but not as piercing. I knew this source-to-sea trip was long and complex, so I had to get restarted or just quit. So there I was, back at it.

The first hour was like a hum-along, but I faked my confidence going downstream and made myself think I was bolder than I was. The water was smooth and uncongested, and I foolishly felt the potential. *Along we go*, I said, and the river obliged without a mood. I noticed it started to widen and add significant turns, which caused me to paddle hard and wide to get across the chasms made by these twists.

The main channel ran efficiently across the corners, but on that day, it was filled with pleasure boats and cruisers. I did not care what anyone said. Kayaks are at the bottom of the river's food chain unless someone rides in a barrel. Cutting across inside or at the far edge of the channel made no difference because paddlers were sitting ducks wherever they went.

It was not my imagination that Lake Pepin's water had turned opaque. This was a new characteristic of the river because the water had always been translucent, regardless of its attitude. The thick Pepin water left a dry and powdery brown smear on everything - my boat, paddle, arms, water boots, and probably some on my face. The river made its stain all over me and my stuff. Maybe it was a badge of courage, but it did not feel like one.

I did not understand the transformation until I noticed the riverbanks were continuous runny mud. Up north, it was mud, but not like this. At least I could stand on it there. Down home, it was warm and sandy. But Pepin's shiny mud ran like a chocolate milkshake, and leached into everything I had in my boat. It sucked out the roots of bankside trees, leaving them like a row of tilting dominoes. Others stood on their unearthed roots, like a witch's bony fingers, unbalanced and threatening to fall.

The water was brown, with no evidence of what was beneath. But this was not the only modification. I was barely accustomed to the heavy water when it started lifting from its bed, not only in one way or in any reliable fashion. First, it came in wavy, an echo of passing speed boats. It rose, then calmed, over and over again. After that, fields of small rolling waves covered the water's surface, running long in both directions, slow and powerful, one after another. They passed me repeatedly. Some larger rollers lumbered through, taking up lots of room. Twice, a tow of barges came slowly around a corner but left hulking rollers anyway. As they arrived, I turned my boat sideways in the river, perpendicular to the rollers, and backed to a small inlet so my bow could penetrate and divide them. This was helpful and diminished the impact of the motion, but afterward, straightening my kayak to get going again took up time, energy, and all my stamina.

I had it learned and implemented confidently when the

wave field changed again. Two and three-foot rollers joined in, some with white caps coming faster. Others were determined to fill my cockpit. If that was not bad enough, I went downstream as the surface energy moved upstream. It was going southeast to northwest, pushing me into a tilt toward upriver, backward from my destination. Every paddle stroke was noticeably more effort than result.

When I decided to take out for a break, I realized there were no boat ramps or solid riverbanks, but everything was covered with riprap, roots, or unapproachable mudslides. The wind and water increased the challenge without warning, and I wondered when I could put my hands up and surrender.

The Mississippi River water was not finished with me. I kayaked nearly twenty-seven percent of its miles but witnessed only a thin skin of its potential. It had a complicated character, and we were not evenly matched, so I wondered how much tenacity I had left.

Despite my determination, the water was more potent and innovative in its natural environment. I could float, though, and it could not. Humans dammed it up, but the water had made new routes. It could evaporate like magic, but I could not. I could drown in water, but the water would never die.

I would not prevail over any battle and would surely lose if I continued to keep score, so I invested in maintaining peace between us. I was floating on an enormous river, wondering if its water would let me through.

Way of Gravity. Before leaving on my kayak trip, I read about a dream when God visited a man through a visualization one night. It was during the hours when people were at home asleep. God opened their consciousness to alert them to reconsider something dreadful they were planning, from a wild and reckless choice, and keep them from the river of no return.

It is not human nature to concede, especially if we have been told to stop what we've already planned. We would do the same, maybe for a child running toward the road. We'd issue a loud, clear warning, then hope they would yield to our concern. But as far as humans go, we do not like to be told by God or anyone.

At the same time, I like the dashboard on my car that warns and informs me about everything I need to know when I need to know it. There is no struggle of will between us about who is right or who's the boss of how it should go. This nocturnal vision is like that, freely downloading warnings for our protection. After reading it before my upcoming river trip, I was left uneasy, but I went anyway.

I want control and think I should have it, just like anyone else, but I usually do not. In town, I control my yard and tree branches, the snow and ice, and the air temperature inside where I live. On the farm, I controlled weeds with chemicals, bugs with more chemicals, and rodents in the barn with poison.

The U.S. Army Corps of Engineers has controlled the Mississippi River for decades, dredging its main channel nine feet down and, in some places, a few hundred feet wide, bordering it with red and green channel markers to keep things in order like a grade school teacher does all day. Wing dams are placed and spaced to control gravity's effect on downward-going water, and colossal locks and dams make steps out of riverbed.

When my mom taught kindergarten, I went to her room and saw a boy with a little piece of masking tape on his lips. She said, *he just wouldn't stop talking.* With the tape, he stopped until he went outside, and the talking started again. That was 1958. But we still have no control over much of anything, even though we are always trying.

True nature changes things constantly while humans persevere like a squirrel at the feeder. We never really win over gravity, and neither does the squirrel. But it remains a constant battle for whoever wants control when no one ever really has it. What control did I find or lose out there on the river? Everything had power over me - a raindrop, a bear, an eighty-barge tow, or a Louisiana hurricane. I stayed on the river for six-hundred fifty miles and then got a lift back home.

CHAPTER 4

Red Tree

I spent the winter season preparing for my journey that was coming in spring when everything would flow again. But I was so distracted I could not stop the thoughts dancing over time and the memories of my life. Even though it was winter, I waited for spring and summer but could only think of autumn.

Just before our bitter winter, summer's vivid colors faded so slowly that I did not notice. The air was warm, and activity persisted while thousands of Sugar Maples that cap our riverside peaks began to secretly change. The cool autumn nights set in motion a decline of chlorophyll that fades warm-weather green. Summer rain and dryness affect the timing, too, but unseen pigments are stirred to promote gaudy colors.

These changes are not bold at first or rattling to us like a sudden blizzard. Neither are they gutsy or blatant, like halos circling the evening moons in the frosty air of October. Our outcrops and crests change colors silently and as slow as a snail's crawl, almost behind our backs. The coming slowdown of winter is surreal if we stay inside too long and do not get a view while it happens. Like craving water in a desert, I longed for colors of other seasons during my one-color winter as I prepared for my kayak trip.

*   *   *

Where I live, fall drips in color as if electrified. Forests on the slopes gradually show yellows as light as pear, then turn bright like lemon and neon, and late-season yellow tomatoes set in the sun. Yellows drift into oranges so brilliantly that a person needs to squint or put on dark glasses. The orange can be as bold as mango fruit or carrot peel before going so vivid and loud, next to the richness of pumpkin skin or ripe peach flesh. Dogwood leaf shows off a deep-berry color, and black gum is even richer than that, like sugar beet tissue or smashed cranberries. When leaves hit the ruby-red level of a pomegranate shell, covering the high peaks along the river, we know it is true autumn here, which feels familiar, just like home.

People from all around come to see it, paying for hotel rooms, food, and parking. But we feel lucky to live in the thick of the spectacle, which we see the first thing and last thing every day, just usually right outside our doors.

The less famous smoke bush is deep in color but more subtle, ethereal, and memorable. My mom's favorite was the mind-blowing red of sumac that grows in clusters on sidelong ditches. Maroon woodbine goes everywhere in yards, not as rich as sumac red, but up brick walls, covers some windows, and over the floor of woods and forest that fence our valley basin. Woodbine likes to crawl quietly and then coil like a yo-yo string, winding up trees or wood poles without anyone noticing until it's too late. Most people don't take the time to tear it down, even if it becomes a nuisance.

All trees and plants turn, but none like our Sugar Maples. Everyone in every region brags about their very own Sugar Maples that are probably all the same, but so loved and fancy that we like to claim them as uniquely ours. When my mom talked about them, it sounded like I must travel home because no other place could have maples like this.

The colors swirl and blend as temperatures and moisture reposition. Light and shade make way for an old, drab winter that I can't stop talking about, maybe like my mom. Once the frost arrives, it goes to nothing. Those tourists go home, artists pack up, grass dries brown, leaves let go and flutter down to clog my gutters, and no more bragging about our exquisite colors. Squirrels and beavers have scrolled up like cochlear, out of sight and behind closed doors of their dreys and lodges. Winter is here, and there is no mistaking it. As I gather my gear, line out some maps, and settle into this long, cold season of preparation, I still have things on my mind. I start to think of my mom.

She was a teacher who began her work in small country schools inland from the Mississippi River and small Iowa riverbanks. Born in West Union in 1927, she routinely taught young students about leaf colors and marveled about them whenever we spoke on long-distance telephone every fall. I learned from her every year that sugar content makes the colors. She said, *the more sugar, the better the color.* She was so excited about it.

Mom loved sharing information about trees and leaves, her home in northeast Iowa in a river town, and the secrets of nature's business. Most topics impassioned her, so she brought them into her classroom and our kitchen at home. She kept a wheelchair at her school for any volunteer to try, *to see how it is to have a difference,* she would say. My mother's stories were about dwindling chlorophyll, sugar in maples, her love for brilliant colors on the river's ridges, and other people's experiences.

My mom was very frugal but impatient for someone to buy her a maple tree one year. When no one did, she bought it herself. She smiled and said, *a Red Maple for Mother's Day* in 1975, as a man planted it inside a white rail fence along a row of arborvitae shrubs. She wanted to see it from her kitchen window. I visited the yard in 2022 and saw the Red Maple in its place forty-seven years later, more significant now after outliving my mother. Its trunk is the diameter and texture of an old-growth tree in a forest, but its height is not the same proportion. It is shorter than a tree with such girth, maybe mimicking my mom's four-foot-eleven-inch stature.

Every day during winter, I assessed kayak gear, sample packing, repacking, weighing, and then doing it again, wishing my mom was here. She was a master organizer and would be a brilliant help to me. I could guess what I might need but did not know what I would really need. So, I did my best to immerse myself in preparation and sank my mind into the randomness of thinking about everything else. The ice and river, sick animals, beautiful nature, the color of leaves, busy and quiet streets, cold weather, wildlife, seasons, family, my mother, my dad, all my family, and everywhere that was ever my home.

Winter moved slowly through. These thoughts came with

it like piles from junk drawers poured out on a bed and over-filled boxes on storage shelves. I emptied them all and looked at every bit of it. Gear loading, mapping, water depths, safety worries, what food, my mother's stories, how much water, long nights out there, the color red, healthy animals, sleeping in the wild, darkness, scary sounds, being alone, growing up, growing old, being me, and how I miss my parents who both died young.

Some of my fears came when it was quiet, some thoughts had no cause, and images were insidious and disturbing. I imagined giant spiders, odd-shaped crunchy bugs, crawling things of all kinds, and curled snakes with slapping tongues straight from movies and fiction. Sometimes, it was about my head in a bear's mouth or an alligator swimming off with an arm or leg that used to be mine. It could be about any other critter sneaking around my tent, breathing heavily, and sniffing for night food. My mind wandered too much as I waited on winter as if I was unpacking and packing all at once.

Everything scary in my thoughts was oversized. I was very tiny in the visions. I imagined almost anything ravaging the goods in my boat while I slept or tearing apart my tent's thin nylon walls to find me inside. I imagined I would be bug-eyed, gripping a flashlight toward its furry face and its mouth showing sharp, shiny animal teeth. I envisioned its surprise when it saw me, an older lady shouting in panic, *are you a friend or a foe?* I often thought about these critters creeping into my camp, crunching stones, and snapping twigs with their padded feet. Obviously, I would know by the weight of the footsteps if they were small, medium, or bear-size. But I know that no animal would ever naturally answer, *I'm a foe!* even if they could talk or had a plan to harm me and my things, no matter what size.

I knew that no human intruder would speak either, and I felt very much alone in these deep meanderings about the river and inside my well-traveled mind. It caused me to wonder how many times, over the many years and nights of sleep since I was born, a spider or centipede crawled over my face or down an arm while I was dreaming securely at home. Or did dormice curl in my elbow and sleep in warmth while I didn't even know it?

If I had a security camera, how often would I see a night intruder pass quietly by my dark window and reach a finger to try the sash? Maybe a hand has gripped the front doorknob and turned, just a try, to see if it was unlocked. I am relieved I have no camera to prove or disprove a truth like that. Then I wondered, *is security an illusion? Is safety we make just a scam? Is sleeping in wild woods alone at night no different than being home?* With these thoughts of a snapping twig outside my tent and a sliding glass pane at my house, I tried to quiet my nerves by talking this way before it actually happened.

Growing up at my childhood home, I slept outdoors often and sometimes below my mom's Red Maple. I was never afraid, yet maybe I should have been for things I did not remember or ever hear about or after a double murder one night when the carnival was in town. All I could think about while yard camping were cows mooing in the distance, a dog's bark at the edge of town, running in the neighbor's yard at three a.m., and my mother's dark red tree. If she was alive now and I spoke of my river fears, she would say, *oh, no, you will be fine. I know you will!* She was exuberant and affirming as she experienced life through every living thing, including me.

Last winter, my adult mind wandered through midnight dread, intensifying to pure shivers. *What will cause my jitters,* I thought so often, *in dark woods along the Mississippi river-banks and sloughs at night or on islands surrounded by endless slurping river water, just me alone with myself?* I was hardly sure how the mythical creatures would approach my dark camp, but they might come from inside my head, me simply scaring myself. Could I stir up such suspense and trepidation beside my boat in a pitch-dark solitary place, so many uncountable miles from home where my family was sleeping? I was frightened already, right here in my bed, with the lights on.

Like my mother's stories, my honest hopes were about peace and enjoyment on the river. Mom's love of the water, lighthouses and tall ships, caves, and natural formations she enjoyed so much, the red color of anything, cardinals, house finches, fall leaves, and spring growth, the red fake carpet she put on her porch steps, was all in my mind and history.

My truth of the river was in these memories, but the fear was in the unknown that loomed beyond my comfort. The scary animals, slimy reptiles, sticky spiders, or other humans out there, I was hoping they would be more afraid of me than I was of them. Fear processing was my way of depleting the night-time thoughts before I got out there, where I hoped to find true peace in real time. This was my hope last winter.

CHAPTER 5

Millie

I told a friend my apprehension over the enormous river trip before me. As it approached, some days quicker than others, I felt shifting points of excitement and hesitation. I examined my life for what impact my going, or failure to return, might have. Humans think the earth will open under the house and suck down everything they put together if their attention is diverted from it. I knew that the thought I put into my forthcoming absence was too much, and it gave excessive meaning to my mere existence and influence.

That same afternoon, I looked around the house to see where my self-importance rested, and there it was. On my dog, Millie. She followed me wherever I went, but it often bothered me. Despite my frustrations with her, I was confident she would miss me the most or be devastated if I did not return from my trip. Then I wondered, *was I deceiving myself?* As dogs go, mine was only average or maybe below, and I had trouble liking her.

In her second year, I realized something was wrong with Millie, which may have caused our tension. As an Australian Shepherd, I applied the breed's typical high intelligence and agility to her, wrongly holding her up to it every day. I did this, and she consistently failed my expectations. I knew I conveyed disappointment in her shortfalls, and I'm sure that she felt she was just not enough.

My first Aussie died after she dug under a fence at the kennel while we were on vacation. She couldn't bear the separation, so she made an ill-fated run for home in the wrong direction during a midnight storm. She was struck by a car and left on the roadside, where we found her after a frantic search when we returned. Months after her death, I decided to look for a new dog.

I read on a breeding site about a female Aussie pup two hours away on a random Sunday, so we loaded up to go for her. When we reached a vast housing development on large rural lots, we envisioned a new garage or basement where this pup was likely weaning. But suddenly, the modern houses ended as we approached an old farmstead hidden behind some scrub and a thick row of bent weed trees.

This was the address, a gravel drive filled with deep ruts and an unpainted barn leaning by the road. High weeds and field grasses grew around everything, including a ramshackle house with broken-out windows and an empty mobile home in a rundown mess. Both were deserted.

Containment yards were fenced with corrugated panels too high to see over, making it difficult to know what was behind. But at intervals, faces of mud-caked livestock peered out as we sat in the driveway. Several rabbit cages sat deep inside a thistle patch near our car, with dozens of bunny ears and eyes evident through the dark shade.

When someone in my car said, *turn the car around and face out*, I knew we all sensed the same need for a quick escape, so I backed around and honked anyway. No one came, so I messaged the man I spoke with, and still, no answer. I waited, honked again, and then exited the car to walk around. The yards were filled with manure and gray-faced old dogs whose teats hung close to the ground. Where there were no weed patches, it was puddled mud, and the air smelled of poorly kept animals and filth.

Eventually, a young woman opened the door of a second trailer house set back from the first. This one had shredded blue tarps as curtains at the windows. She hollered as she started down the porch steps, but I was unsure if it was at me or the dark brown puppy bouncing after her. When she approached, she shouted that her husband was in the fields, but she could sell the dog to me. As she spoke about it endearingly, the brown puppy ran past us into the deep grass until I could only see its tail tip.

The woman was rotund or pregnant, without shoes, and wearing a dirt-covered teeshirt pulled tightly over a too-small dress. Despite the surrounding conditions, she seemed happy enough. She explained that this was their last pup as if she wanted to increase my enthusiasm to have it. At the same time, I glanced behind her and saw the pup's tail rising wildly from the weed patch, so I pardoned myself as I rounded the seller and headed toward the dog. The tail hair was thick and bushy for a small puppy, like a teenager's billowy ponytail.

The brown fur was dense and beautiful but dotted with dirt and chunks of debris stuck deep inside it.

The long tail had an odd right-angle tilt at the center but wagged forcefully, energetic like a horsetail swatting flies. When I reached for the puppy, it did not dart from me because it was focused on eating a mound of fresh horse manure like it was served just for her. As she gulped it, I touched her tail. After she yelped and yanked away in pain, I realized it had been broken. It dangled at the bend, appearing like the farmer was unsuccessful when he tried to dock it.

I picked up the puppy, held her to my chest, and mentally noted how she pushed all four paws hard against me, determined to get down. It was unlike any puppy I had known, as she braced like a stubborn child, and she smelled stale. This little dog was way past starving and desperate to return to the manure pile.

The conditions were horrific for the pregnant old dogs, the little brown pup, and the farm animals glaring from behind the barricades. The human dwellings looked as bad. Maybe even worse and a good enough reason to sell off land to new housing developers. Despite my concerns about the puppy's condition, I paid two hundred dollars and left quickly. We stopped directly at a nearby farm store for puppy food and water.

I named the dog Millie, not after the puppy mill where she was born, but for a white-haired woman I knew as a child. Mildred grew marigolds near her porch and down the walkway, attracting many bees. The flowers gave off a friendly aroma that reminded me of berry-picking with my grandma and gave me a lifelong love for the marigold scent. My grandma called the woman Millie since they were old friends, and between them, I felt included and cared for just after I was mostly orphaned.

I wanted Millie as our farm dog, so the money was adequate to pay. But it was fifteen hundred more dollars at the vet to cure her various worms, giardia, coccidia, and mites. She suffered from urinary problems, constant diarrhea, kidney issues, nervousness surpassing any human, and lifelong pain at the tail bend. Months after continuous doctoring, Millie dug her heels in and was home to stay. Then, my high hopes rose against her as I unwittingly compared her to my first and best Aussie. When I marked Millie's name on her paper file, I saw that I wrote *Millie, #2.* I should have known then that something was up. My compassion for her was deep, but I didn't like her very much.

While waiting for my launch date, I observed Millie more closely. She whined a lot, typical from the first day I brought her home. She vocalized about everything, whimpered to go outside too often, and then did not even try to pee once we got out there. When whining wasn't enough, she embellished it with a tipped head and wrinkly face, which escalated to a paw on my knee and a few sharp barks. Her incessant needs and desires cycled through her dog world with the urge to pee, maybe poo, look around, drink water, sniff flowers, eat some food, watch the neighbor, get petted, lay down, sit up, walk around, then all over again. And she wouldn't do any of it alone.

The whines came in jagged little screeches, then one long unbearable yell, a steady whimper, and sometimes, a staring contest with loud barks. The cycle was endless, proving our vet right - *a needy dog was as intolerable as an aggressive dog.*

Millie continued to monopolize the household at the farm and then at our new home in town. If we could ignore her long enough, she occasionally tired of herself and switched to friendly cat chasing, a noisy and clumsy pursuit narrated with constant high-pitched, staccato barks. Nothing calmed or distracted Millie from her need to be the center of attention.

I imagined my dog in the kayak, on a river, or camping in the woods, but I realized I was expecting too much from her again. I felt brokenhearted when I imagined Millie alone, wandering along the shore or lost in the woods after running fearfully from my night camp on a riverbank. It troubled me to envision her swept downstream in a panic after leaping from my boat. I knew she couldn't come along on my river trip. She would never be a kayak-riding dog, but I wished she was different. Millie was not that kind of dog, and we both knew it.

It was common for Millie to walk into things and then yelp after she did it. We tested her eyesight, and the vet suspected dog glaucoma, but there was nothing we could do about it, he said. The doctor criticized her because she was a problematic handful, and nothing would change her neediness whatever we did. But when he touched her, he was gentle and always whispered, *yes, you're a friendly dog, aren't you?* He was right. Her heart was big, and she only wanted what she would never feel – comfort.

I tried to train Millie as we worked together to achieve the impossible. During her first year, she focused enough to learn some essential things. I taught her to look at me on command at three months old while she was becoming healthy. She understood and could do it when asked for the rest of her life.

The reinforcement was uncomplicated, and the training bonded us. But Millie could not develop higher-level training tools or chained skills because she lived only in moments. Still, she proved she was at least smarter than a chicken. Millie's attention span was short, she was easily distracted, and her neurology was random.

Millie excelled when I used a basic manners and attention span program. However, her ability to hold memory and behaviors was unreliable. My family and I ran Millie through our walking trails and pastures on the farm daily, but the drain in energy lasted only as long as it took to get her back to the house. Our farm vet continued offering to put her down, reminding me that *a needy dog is as troublesome as an aggressive dog* and that she would never change. Millie's new groomer held back a complaint when she said, *Millie yelps and wails* throughout her bath-and-cut. But she did not include Millie on the noisy bad dog list that troubled the groomer's neighbors, though I was sure Millie was on it.

My pervasive disappointment in Millie caused me to miss something. She loved me. Her connection to me was like gum stuck on a shoe. She was hurt if I failed to greet her or forgot a morning pat. The hurt in her eyes disappeared when I gave her affection. Millie never forgot what she felt for me, but my disappointment persisted.

I hired a trainer to teach me techniques and expectations that might help Millie. We worked together for years, but it rarely brought lasting change. I made a list of positives and negatives to clarify the problems, whether it was me or Millie, and it gave me something concrete when I was about to give up. Twenty-five points on the good list - Millie understood and obeyed many spoken words, *wait, sit, touch* – how she behaved in the house, her loving nature, and gentleness with children or strangers. When Millie approached a flower garden or just a patch of dandelions, she methodically sniffed each one, petal by petal, something humans have little patience in doing. Millie pushed her full face into snow and stayed there for a minute or two before coming out, white-covered and joyful.

On the con list was her excessively high anxiety, which contributed to most of her negatives. Millie's distress increased over the months despite the cocktail of sedatives and calmers she took daily. Of course, fireworks, sirens, and screeching cars were bothers, but then people talking, a knock at the door, a squeaky chair, and something so slight that only a dog could hear it set her off into hours of trembling and worry.

A humane society report said puppy mill dogs have a six to eight times greater chance of scoring high ranges of fearfulness. They often become overly attached but cannot benefit from extra attention or soothing. Separation anxiety and obsessive-compulsive behaviors were heightened in puppy mill dogs, just as they did for Millie. Tedious behaviors, an overwhelming low rate of trainability and coping with everyday existence, altered mental function, and difficulty dealing with stress, anxiety, and noises were all listed in the report and familiar to our household with Millie. Additional research corroborated these findings and my deep-seated disappointment with my dog.

I continued to negotiate Millie as my river companion. My

ambiguity frustrated me whenever I realized my desire could not be grasped, not with this dog. But she was the dog I had, my dog. I wondered if I was selfishly mitigating isolation on my river trip by putting it on Millie, even if just in my mind. I was tormenting both of us with my unacceptance of who she was and who she could not be. I hated my disappointment in something I loved.

Eventually, while I prepared for my long trip on the river, I looked at Millie through the lens of our absence from each other, which caused me to see her differently. I had made her something she was not, which caused her to fail me every day. But I had failed her, as well, by not accepting her for who she truly was. My dog, Millie, was not unintelligent or unable to do many things. She lacked focus, loved mischief, and ate whatever was on the floor, even if it belonged there. She was an imperfect doofus, a knucklehead, and a troublemaker who accepted me despite my disappointment and desire that she was different. Her neurology was broken, and there was nothing that she nor humans could do to fix it. As she worsened, I accepted that it wasn't me, our relationship, or Millie. It was humans at the puppy farm that did this.

I wanted Millie to ride with me on my long river trip, to be my companion, but I knew she would need all the room in my mind, boat, and heart. She would need excessive food I could not carry and whine for whatever was out of reach. I did not know what would trigger her anxiety or how she would react to anything. Would she attempt to play with a bear, kill a rabbit, roll in the river, or cry all night? The images of her lost in the woods or rushing downstream after jumping overboard became more prevalent.

I had to face it. Millie did not measure up as a kayak-riding dog. I wanted her to lay in my camps at night, watching over things and quietly guarding me and our stuff against unknown creatures. But Millie never barked at a noise or scared a stranger at home, only licked visitors soppy and wiggled with delight, whether an outsider or not. I had to stop thinking she would be our protector in the wilderness.

In time, Millie's over-excitability transitioned to panic and shivering that lasted hours once it was triggered. Hitting a rumble strip when riding in the car, nearby railroad noises, sirens, any bangs or slams, and the monthly civil defense test set her nerves on fire every time. It lasted hours, then evolved to days until it became her constant state. She had two comfy beds and an indoor crate to hide, but the worry never left her eyes. The vacuum, blender, electric drill, or music – eventually, nothing was tolerated. We gave her hugs, a thunder coat, hemp oil, daily calming bites, massages, white noise, fluoxetine, and an endless combination. The sedation aids caused stomach upset and foaming, especially during panicky times, and nothing circumvented Millie's troubles that were so deep in her neurobiology.

Millie loved her illusive comfort and longed for it unceasingly. I imagined her wet or muddy, cold and tired on the river trail, and I knew she could not endure it. Millie would be too much for me, and the river would be too much for her, so I surrendered my desire and said she should stay home.

I was always assured of Millie's heart. It was also unceasing, flowing from honey-colored eyes, staring intensely at me. From her tail when it wagged too much as I walked in a room and her unkempt self when she bumped into me every time I passed her, I could not find our harmony. I know now I was angry that I loved her, and loving her was complicated, difficult, fruitless, and draining. I see you now, Millie, near me in heart and spirit, remembering, loving, and seeing what was buried inside. She was innocent.

Millie stayed home. If I didn't return, I knew she'd miss me. If I did return, I knew she'd be waiting. And she was. Then I dreamed Millie was a giant mouse wearing a dog leash with a broken grip. In the dream, Millie spoke to tell me a man attacked her. But I didn't believe her.

Millie
July 7, 2018 – October 20, 2022

CHAPTER 6

Free

I had a dog named Maggie, a hundred-pound golden retriever. I walked her twice a day, any day year-round. She nosed the ground in zigzags and loops all summer, taking me between houses, through alleys, and under tall shrubs. We trespassed, jaywalked, opened gates, and hoped not to get caught when we veered off city sidewalks. I wondered what was haywire in Maggie because her incessant trailing seemed useless.

When winter arrived and new snow covered the ground, Maggie continued her madness but with more enthusiasm because she loved the cold. She pulled me all over our north-side neighborhood and did not care what others thought. But now it made perfect sense in the light layer of snow.

Raccoon footprints, squirrel tracks, other canines, human prints, deer, cat trails, and mouse paths were now evident in the snow. Maggie's nose picked up the scent of their weaving all along, but now, as she traced, I understood the connections. Her name, retriever, explained it. It was no longer senseless when I realized her genetic inclination was nosework for dogs.

Writing now, I am like Maggie. I am following the scent from one story to another. What might seem unrelated are memories of my life, alone and with others, young or older, for all seasons over many decades, on the river or at home. These might be ramblings to some, but they are connected by common threads, weaving me and the things I have loved and experienced. It is human nosework.

It was the winter before my river trip and months after the idea to paddle the Mississippi came to me. Before I could get on the river, many more months would pass through the wintery season. During that time, I could barely keep up with my mind saturated with thought and anticipation. Like skipping stones over water, I tossed it onto paper to make some order of my mental piles.

*   *   *

Training in my boat was impossible because the river was solid in nearby sloughs and waterways. Open water was rare, and ice-over was averted only in shallow rushing streams. Besides this, the cold made fluid water unsafe to go out alone. It was my friend Heather who asked if I wanted to go after she found Coon Creek open and coursing through Vernon County. The water there was swift with ice-shelf growing toward the center, but eddies and underflow were not yet frozen hard.

We were quietly giddy that day. It was cold as a witch kiss when we met in the parking near the creek, where the air hung heavy and intimidating. Despite being dressed in dense layers, the bitey temperature crept through our cold-weather gear. We did it anyway, dropped our kayaks into rushing water, jumped on board, and let the water rush take us. Our activity drew sightseers along the creek road above as we sped downstream, hardly a paddle placed but only to steer. A daring jogger stopped to stare, only for a minute, and an older couple in a pickup lowered the window to take a picture. Maybe our two boats in speeding ice water, two women southbound in a snow-fringed creek, was peculiar for their day. But it was just an unprotested and inevitable adventure, a fait accompli for Heather and me.

Pools of rapids spun us like compass needles, but we continued upright and dry. After a quarter mile or less and a range of close calls, Heather pointed to a rocky take-out where water was pooling and circling before it gained speed to twist off downstream through Hamburg and over Koll Valley. It wiggled tightly toward Chaseburg with a sharp switchback before dipping under Mill Street to eventually deplete into the Mississippi River, miles to the south and west. Across the creek ahead ran barbed fencing, stretched from west bank to east, separating farmers from summer grassland and holding Angus on their fields.

Above us, near the take-out, was a steep but short slope that angled to an asphalt path. We dragged our boats on snow along the rising trail to reach Old Mill Road, where we squirreled our kayaks behind a crusty rim and walked back to our vehicles. We loaded up, headed back home to thaw, and never denied the risk we took. This was a dangerous but remarkable kayak ride on a bone-chilling Sunday.

* * *

Stuck at home the rest of winter, apprehension and enthusiasm hovered over me. How things would go when I paddled hundreds of river miles through the summer was a mystery. During winter in the Mississippi River Valley, the wait was slow while our pool eight remains solid from brutal arctic air. The landscape becomes barren here and stony gray in dormant monotony like a black-inked etching on copper. The valley's hibernation was harsh and piercing in the center of every cold season. Winter by the water is noticeable compared to more subtle seasons blending in our river town. I could not stop thinking about spring and the warm summer ahead and felt restless.

All living things, human and animal, are more evident in warmer seasons because they make noise and seek provisions when days are long and more pleasant. Movement and friction generate aromas and heat, while these energize and drive the force of our city. Cascading traffic on bluff roads, footpaths, and neighborhood streets is in constant motion, sandwiched between twin ridges bordering the valley where it builds up pressure.

Nonstop ants on their trails intentionally track the pheromones that keep them knit together. These little red creatures seek kitchens, our crumbs, and drippings off the floor as night animals traipse around the marshes and ridgetops where humans walk only in the day. Some critters track into yards below at night to see what we left on our decks or in the garbage.

*   *   *

My mind drifts to a summer afternoon when a little orange mammal deviated down the sidewalk by my house, obviously lost from its hole, now in the center of town. As it got closer, it became clear. It was a mangy red fox that looked like it got a haircut from another fox using dull scissors and no mirror. Its orange tufts were surrounded by bare, reddened skin, and its tail was gauzy and ragged with a betraying droop. The fur remained unkempt and tangled from its relentless scratching meant to deaden the intrusive crowd of burrowing scabby mites. A once beautiful and self-reliant fox seeking relief wandered the neighborhood. It was innocent but disoriented and frantic after being plagued and made helpless by a tiny parasite.

A story comes to mind of Shepherd, our farm llama who protected the sheep flocks night and day for most of his life. He was brown in color, profound and pure as dark Brazilian coffee beans, with a neck that reached six feet above the ground where he stood. His eyelashes looked false and thick with mascara and swept upward like he used a lash curler. And his grandness was balanced only by his devotion to watch over our sheep and his claim they belonged to him. He always looked down on us as lesser humans.

When Shepherd was offloaded from his seller's truck, we penned him below the barn where he could see the sheep without access. I thought it might be days for him to become acquainted with his home and new responsibilities. But at once, he eyed the sheep across the back pasture and, without twitching, opening his lips, or rippling his throat, he emitted a whole-body bawl like an alphorn echoing across the acres, meant to attract and claim his animals.

Shepherd was top-grade at work and gave us secure sleep, night after night, for years. His tolerance for spring lambs sliding from his back as he sunned caused us to stop work to enjoy their play and his patience. He sat tall and majestic until he was done. Then, like any grandpa who had enough, he tipped them off into a pile and walked away.

As I packed my kayak and assembled gear over winter, my mind continued to wander. I recalled tragedy when I thought of industrious animals, the decrepit fox, our sheep, the llama, and what happened next. I fenced in the woods the summer before to increase shady pasture and improve flock management. Shepherd tended to the woods flock and came to the barn when he tailed the ewes as they followed my grandchild and me after dark.

One day late in the second woods summer, he sat in the sheep room, head high as usual, chewing cud and staring at me while I cleaned the barn. Seemingly relaxed, I assumed he was dodging his sheep-tending to avoid the heat of the baking sun.

The following day, I found Shepherd in the same place but hobbled and weak, unable to rise. He showed no interest in eating the hay and grain I gave, and this defied his usual hardy appetite. Two hours later, he rested his long neck across the floor as if yielding to something he could not explain. Too feeble to recover, I found him dead that late evening.

This and the later deaths of many prolific ewes alarmed us as we feared what killed Shepherd and ran through our barns. It was the brain worm, an insidious and sickening parasite that lives in the head of the whitetail deer and whose larvae are spread in the woods by slugs. A stomach-churning feeling rises when an animal minds its business and is killed anyway. This happens to humans, too.

As the distracted fox passed my yard, it gave a side glance but continued urgently with no apparent plan, a sign of an animal in duress. The llama, our sheep, the fox, and a frog I found dead stirred my memory of a skunk whose face was stuck in a plastic bottle as it wandered in circles near the road. I pulled over but could not help before I lost it behind a farmer's barn.

I cannot erase them from my mind, sick and inflicted animals who unnaturally visit in daylight against their instinct or better judgment. But it makes sense when raccoons, possums, feral cats, sharp-shinned hawks, foxes, and a woodchuck go off-course. I have seen them all.

A black bear was in town, some white-tail deer, and a saw-whet owl stared at me one night from a white pine where I stood making a wood fire. Some evening bats aimed at my flashlight, a bobcat wanting a way into the hen house, and a great horned owl, maybe looking for a distressed skunk with its head in a bottle. A pileated woodpecker shrieked at me in the yard one early morning recently. It is when our worlds overlap, or we get lost and meander out of our territory.

The warmer months prove life and its direction, everything with proper or explainable purpose, until winter's slowdown begins to smolder, and we all go inside. There's something wrong with those who stay out wandering in ill-suited light, naively lunching on contaminated things that make them sick. Their weakness and lack of wisdom cause death or rampant illness in deep winter.

*   *   *

I am thinking of summer now. My mind jumped. It was the first winter before my river trip, but now what rose in my mind was about summer after. As it was, summer came, and I went on my kayak trip as planned. The nights were my favorite times, and places of rest were beautiful and welcoming. I favored tent sleeping, solitude in the dark, and distant river camping as I looked forward to it every day. The gigantic creatures of my haunted imaginings did not exist, or at least did not bother me at all. The time was friendly, and animals were busy minding themselves as we shared the wild space while I trespassed in their realm.

An earthen mound the size of a milk cow was home to thousands of black ants that drew a bear into my camp off a marshland. I was curious whether they were in my space or I was in theirs. But I always knew they were there first. The bear came for ants, and ants bit the bear and me, just wanting to sleep and be left alone. I hoped the bear stayed away all that night, but if it came, it was for the ants because my food bag was undisturbed.

Back at home, still winter, the dreads finally calmed as the season crawled. I was uneasy about how things would go when paddling, carrying gear, finding night spots, making food, and navigating it alone. But enthusiasm and excitement intervened, and I was eager to get going by May. So I continued to pack and become familiar with my gear, like the Big Agnes insulated and orange sleep pad that reduced to a pop-can size when unused. The evolution sleep quilt of the lightest down, with a sewn-in foot pocket for cold toes and a hood for chilly nights, was in eggplant color, which helped me want it from the dent-and-bent section of a nearby gear company. My Wise Owl pillow was too bulky to be practical, but I took it along anyway. These three kept me too sleepy to be afraid through any night. I loved sleeping out there.

On a particular summer night, I was in deep comfort, grateful while I slept in this almost wake-filled dream that a rare planetary alignment was coming. Visible to any long-distance paddler through this particular weekend made it extra exciting. During this last week of June, Mercury, Venus, Mars, Jupiter, and Saturn were all in the morning sky. The exact alignment would only happen again when I am too old to sleep on Big Agnes, in 2040, when I will be eighty-six. Yet no one knows what I might be doing, not even me. It would be magical and extraordinary if I were out there, old and unsteady, sleeping sound on Big Agnes below planets aligning and tinselly stars.

One night, I could hear the river water a few meters from my tent. It slurped against the bank in a quiet, reassuring, and irregular swishing. I feared this during winter at home, but I loved it when it came that summer. Because of the sounds, I was soothed into an unfamiliar peacefulness not often felt and none of the fright I had anticipated.

While thinking about this during my sleep, something started hitting me on the head. It was not rock-hard but firm and bland, like an angry cat's tail. I wondered what it could be, this thing silently tapping until I woke. Then I knew. The wind, coming in nearly twenty mph blows, had caused my tent to tremble rhythmically like a tail thumping me out of sleep as it tapped on the crown of my head.

Could the aligning planets cause this wind to rattle? My thoughts switched to the strength of my tent. This cheap little Night Cat was a favorite but awkwardly designed too tall for a pod shelter. I got it half-priced when the total price was already reasonable. That night, it caught the wind while I slept until I thought we would sail into the air, up over the river where the water surface was full of rollers and white caps, even though it was too dark to see. Should I have left the tent before it went airborne? By staying, I weighed it down for me to turn in my quilt and return to sleep.

Ultimately, I missed the planetary alignment because I was so comfortable. Suddenly, I felt concerned I couldn't kayak that next day in high winds. I felt the onset of rumination at two a.m. Would I be too old to sleep outside in 2040? Was I going to levitate in my cheap tent under my quilt and soar over the river in darkness lit only by this rare layout of planets? Should I have brought this clunky pillow? And what about that next day? Would I even be able to travel a windy river? It was then two twenty-one a.m., and the winds were letting up. Was it enough to experience this moment and the next, for the first time, and go back to sleep? I felt a powerful spirit in me and all around, one I could leave things to while I rested.

I did not think about how good it could be during my winter worries. But I heard bullfrogs moaning and a train in the distance, and then I realized it: I was free. This is much better than my made-up scares, recoiling in fear, and suspected intrusions by odd creatures. In real life, light, color, quiet, solitude, and peace were truths that came at night.

By morning, the water was shiny and flat, giving me the urge to ice skate over it as if I were young. The current was nearly undetectable and streaming with gravity for a change, going downriver without a gripe. The sky was mildly blue, with no cloud action. It was just not a dramatic time. I should not even write about something so plain and benign. It was a zero on a ten-point scale.

When I began my trip after the long, dragged-out winter, I asked to be spared one thing. It was fear. Anything wrapped with anxiety would be ruined. Dread was like the bug net I had capped over my head due to morning gnats. Even though I was protected from that day's hatch, everything I saw had a layer of white net between it and me. Like the net, fear influences everything, even an ideal zero morning. So, my desire to be free of fear was granted to make more room for truth.

After winter and into my trip's start, I felt much more, like when I thought the water betrayed me or I sunk into mean-hearted mud that had it out for me. I felt hurt, but it was only mud. Nothing on my kayak trip had feelings but me. I felt disappointed, frustrated, cautious, exuberant, inexperienced, excited, and blessed. My day was a simple day on a slow-moving river. Gnats weren't annoying, the wind was not blowing, and the trees were quiet. And I felt free.

CHAPTER 7

Float

This is about my Delta kayak, made by people who believe in its design, technology, and composition from Maple Ridge. It was tested in the water of a river near where it was made. I believe in what they create, just as they do, especially after living in my boat on the river for two months.

Much of Delta's end design is done by hand, so with that and other strategic perfections, I consider a Delta kayak as close to precision as human effort can achieve. But this is only an opinion, and I am unfairly biased because I am confident in the manufacturer's work. Without being preoccupied with unearned and embarrassing pride, the Delta team can put all its energy and intellect into its impressive product rather than ego, false achievement, or any conceit.

The boat speaks for itself. In a cherry red color and plastics technology, my boat is a blend with an ABS opaque polymer base layer and Solarkote surface that will never biodegrade, fortunately, and regrettably. Its desirable features, advanced design, and thermoform construction do nothing to make it sacred. But its primary purpose is to make travel efficient, more comfortable, and possible. It flows over and sits on water when quiet, making it highly valuable.

I discovered this Delta briefly after my paddling idea came to me in late summer 2021 while I was at the paddle dealer assessing touring and performance kayaks. Someone told me that a person could not go on a long trip in a recreational kayak, but I thought that they could and probably had done it, but it would take forever. The gear load might produce an unevenness that could risk a flip and reduce stability. Despite the usual stability of recreational kayaks, they are not ordinarily intended or designed to carry what is needed on long trips.

Wasted energy also builds from endless micro-switchbacks while tracking for hundreds of miles or even much less. A full-scale side-to-side waddle alternates from the bow to the stern, particularly at the front. This is mostly absent from a touring kayak, so a paddler is less fatigued at the end of the day and can complete many more miles on a same-length trip.

I admit I made a mistake at the paddle store. I let myself be convinced that a Daggar Stratus 12.5s was the right kayak for me without carrying it on land or first riding it on water. It was because of my ever-willingness to listen to the opinions of others more often than my own, at least in some situations. Once I arrived home, I knew it was too clunky for me and too coarse to manage out of water despite its ability to glide naturally on a river or pond.

Three days later, I drove a hundred miles to return it without paddling it on the backwaters near my house. During that second visit, I floated two boats on a slimy green pond out back and just north of an outflow near a nine springs creek.

The first boat on the water was an appealing ultralight, graphite black, so light I could see through the hull at some angles, tilting my head just right. It was a canoe-kayak hybrid that I could pick up and move with one hand, without gear, and while empty. With a vacuous and reverberating interior like the bell of a sousaphone, it had no seat, foot pedals or compartments, neither shock cord nor bungees, no clips on portal covers, in fact, no hatches at all, and entirely unlike the fully-equipped Delta that sat right next to it.

This ultralight was one ample and open space, unlike the Delta, which had all the attachments, separate hatches, and more. If that wasn't worrisome enough, the ultralight's hull was so deep that my head barely rose over the coaming in any direction I turned. I felt like a tadpole in a five-gallon bucket. It was not fun or safe despite its lean specs proving I could handle it. Being able to lift a boat without the ability to paddle it defeats its purpose. The reverse is also true and confirmed by so many kayaks that I can paddle but barely budge on the ground.

The second boat I tested was one I saw on my first visit three days before, and I wanted it then. After all that, I decided to buy it and was delighted with my decision and the boat. I drove home with the Delta 15s on my car top, a fifteen-foot length, twenty-two inches at the center, and 's' to signify a smaller stature person.

This boat had a little more cost for being light, longer, and accessorized, but it was not as lightweight as the ultra-lite black that felt like I was clomping in my dad's big shoe. My

Delta was forty pounds, enabling me to lift it with little or no help, at least when empty. The 's,' along with the forty-pound feature, caused me optimism and trust toward this boat, good since it would be home for me and all my stuff for many days on the river.

Back at my house, I tested the notion of a tour or performance kayak versus the recreational style. When I had my Pelican Mustang on the water southeast of the backwaters I frequent, I stroked with all my might to travel a certain distance. Even though I gave it my all, the Mustang went just two and a half mph, maybe three, once or twice. This boat is clunky but comfortable, like a favorite slipper, and with remarkable and reassuring stability engineered into it. You could rapidly tap dance in it or twirl around, which is exaggerating, but you would definitely remain upright on a windless and peaceful day.

On a second day, I did the same run with similar water in my touring kayak and found myself efficiently doing five mph with little effort, sometimes six with equal energy, so twice as fast or more. Figuring it, the same action could get a long trip done in half the time riding a touring performance kayak.

I learned quite a lot on my days testing my two boats. A touring boat differs significantly from a recreational kayak, even though both have their purpose and place. The amount of gear stowed on a long trip would not fit in my Mustang, and if I worked at cramming it, the boat would likely be cumbersome on the river and quickly turn over. I see it turning on its own like a hog on a spit or, even quicker or worse, twirling like the earth on its axis at peak velocity, erratic and warped. A planet picks up leap seconds as it spins too fast and then too slow, and humans must reset its balance. My imagination sees the Pelican turning like this. Fat and stout, recreational boats are best for day travel or an overnight, maybe just some equipment, but I am still wary. Calmer water, but not the Mississippi's main channel, is friendlier to these stocky and stable boats.

The other drawback is that the boat is without those hatches. Their lids are loose like untied hats, different from the tight-as-Tupperware lids with double-rubber gaskets and bungee-latch hooks on the Delta and other touring models. As I said, this is not bragging, but I wonder about all this as I write. But still, the recreational boat is good, just suited for its own activities.

Besides speed and waterproof storage space, with stability as its crucial and given factor, the touring kayak had another outstanding quality I loved. I learned about it exhaustively from my daily experience on the river. The build was purposeful after considering cutting ability through all types of water.

I was mesmerized many afternoons as the upswept bow of my Delta sliced through surface rollers, waves, and boilers, unlike any recreational boat I had ever paddled. It left me dry at most essential times, and my cockpit did not become a giant dishpan of dirty water by the end of a day. The skeg held me straight from twisty wind and underwater push while working in unison with the upturned bow. These features are usually missing from a recreational kayak but are crucial on a big river like the Mississippi.

The cockpit seat is where I spent hours of daily paddling time. It was designed with channel venting and core drainage to pull water off and down away from me. I usually felt amazingly comfortable with the multi-position seat and its back adjustment abilities. This is not an advertisement but the truth I have experienced myself. It was an exceptionally well-planned package of comfort, safety, and efficiency that did not disappoint me. I loved it more as I went each day.

My kayak is designed like a Bank Swallow skimming the water and created with precision. The swallow shows off a little with its skill to swoop like a musician gliding over piano keys. I could never do it alone. Once, I tried using ropes with a sail out over the ocean and nearly killed myself. I can't glide over water unless I am in my boat. Likewise, the boat cannot do it without me. The Delta can skim like this even over the slightest smoothness of shallow water and the craggy top of rough water, but only with me and a paddle.

That cord-operated skeg helped my aim go straight like an arrow set on a string. If I were a bird, I could get there by resisting the wind, like a falcon's sharpness, but I needed a skeg. A raptor is the envy of other birds because it can glide even in the most reckless and pushy wind, like my rope-with-sail contraption, but they can do it freeform and fancy without all the gadgets.

It is settled. The boat is good, but am I? It takes both of us, I know. This good boat and I are headed downstream on an enormous river that people call the Mighty Mississippi and Big Muddy – I am not sure what to think, and I don't know what will happen.

The Delta kayak had been in my garage since the 2021 winter set in late. I felt pleased about having it, but when I walked by, I sensed how ignorant I was about whether it would work for me on this long and upcoming mystery trip. I took it on back channels and the main, time and again before the winter freeze, but I did not feel at home or proficient on those later-season days when the river was rock-solid ice, and I was forced only to imagine. Floating across thawed water was only a thing in my mind by then.

On one of my pre-winter local trips, I took a picnic bag for an eight-mile slog when the water was still wet and moving. This experience, eating lunch on the water and in solitary quiet, caused me to love my boat and grow to trust it. Neither I nor it could go anywhere without the other. That was clear. So far, during that hardened winter, which eventually came and stayed for months, I could only wonder how all this would go when things melted, and I began paddling. Whether it was a good or bad idea, it was not something I could know that soon.

*   *   *

As my gear load expanded over winter months, accumulating and sorting, I read over and again the Delta manual that said *this performance touring kayak has a one-and-a-half gallon day hatch, seventeen-gallon bow hatch, a twenty-seven-gallon stern hatch, and a maximum load capacity of two hundred seventy pounds,* which I knew included me. By then, it was plain impossible for me to convert hatch gallons to piles of supplies and equipment of various shapes and sizes, although I had been stewing over it for the months of winter.

Minus me from the two-hundred-seventy pound capacity only allowed for a few extra or indulgent heavy items. I decided to spend those crusty months of winter assembling what I could only imagine necessary, but by that next spring, I would take the boat off the garage wall to fit my actual needs.

This was the only way for me to eyeball the ratio of gallon equivalence to pieces of gear.

Packing was just so difficult to know. Was it okay to take only one bar of soap, no hairbrush at all, but yes to five pounds of fresh ground coffee and a large sack of Lindt chocolate balls? How tricky a chore it was. As it turned out, I learned the hard way. Bagged chocolate does not survive the midday sun on a boat, but fresh ground coffee was good as gold every morning and even better with runny chocolate added. I never needed a hairbrush, but I was always happy to have my soap.

Ultimately, I loaded too heavy despite my simplifying reductions dozens of times over my work at it. At least three times while traveling, I thinned my gear and sent home unused or bothersome items in my family's car or a mailed box from the Northwoods. During a holiday visit home, I unloaded another amount of pointless weight and bulk, all very common to a first-time long-distance trip.

In the end, my gear weight fell below a critical mass that enabled me to manage more simply as I learned my needs. This reduced my stress the rest of my time on the river, despite going without some comforts and conveniences. During this trip, I knew everything would take place with the boat or in it, except night camping at sites unknown, on sandbars, islands, or an accessible riverbank or small-town park. Everything I needed or wanted was with my Delta kayak, except for one major exception.

When I longed for ice on the hot river many sweltering days, it was not in my boat. I wanted the cold so much that I almost drank the river and could not stop thinking about something frozen. One rare day after I found an ice machine on a marina dock in Iowa, I bought ten pounds of bagged cubes to crunch through the afternoon on my downstream paddle. The bottled water onboard was by then like bathwater, warm and unpleasant, and even though it hydrated all right, it did not quench or sustain me. The ice bag dripped in the sun as I crunched, melting down my arm over the rest of me. I hadn't thought so highly of simple ice until that day.

Often, I felt like an amateur, sloppy with ignorance and no good sense to even be out there even though I had a good boat. I sometimes felt foolish with no leading edge to certify me to be the one to go. My boat was not angelic or special in the elevated spiritual sense, just as I'm not special either. The opposite of me is holiness and of some other human spirit. My boat and I were ordinary and had to work together to rise up. Who I was when I left and who I became can not be credited to me or my boat. It was something much bigger. But I was the benefactor of the blessing.

A divineness of life was in the air around me and all things, over the water, in it, through my experience of it and me just doing it, over me and in me at times. The ability to change is extraordinary and out of the human realm, indeed not made by me, but the willingness comes directly from humans. It isn't in thermoplastics, microplastics, or a lone person's limited knowledge or weakness. In muscles or glands, the lobes and air sacs, midribs and petioles of leaves and greens, organics and nutrients of the earth, and microbes, molecules, or bacteria that make up a simple water drop. It is purely spiritual, just as the ordinariness of science. It is what enabled me to float on water. I did not produce it, but it is what I saw, not what I transported with me, but how it moved me. It is the supernatural.

The sacredness of Earth and air is perfect, a pervasive spirit and otherworld of day and night, all of it, physics of movement on the water, over the water, floating, rising, gliding, changing places minute by minute, being carried and watched over. It is more excellent consistently, over all of time, never relying on me for it or for anything.

Riding in this boat down an ever-changing, moving, and full river, it was just me, this boat, my stuff, and survival, floating, and thinking. I am a speck. The God I want would be unambivalent, an unambiguous spirit, or I would not go out there to travel and see the marvels of it and to sleep next to my boat listening to river splash at night, under the sky, moving stars, auras, or then to rise, or never to make it home, anything could have been its end, my end.

Humans are weak and shapeless, but as spirits, we are evident, uplifted, inspiring, or giants. It is within all possibilities for every human. This is hope. I was buoyed up and encouraged, not because of my boat, no, because of the inexpressible. But without my Delta, I still would not have gone out there.

I am clear that I am the reliant and needful one. Even tipping out of my boat, nearly drowning, preparing to breathe the water, to drench my lungs, but rising back up, rushed downstream, and rescued, it is not of me. It's not my doing but a combination of so many things outside of me and from another realm, one that can make things happen that shouldn't happen if based on our human reasoning. So then we say, oh, that's a miracle because we don't know any better.

Everything was happening without say from me. Humans

only borrow wisdom and strength, only pretend and hope to know, but none is originally ours. Humans lose freely-given things every day, like children and their lunch money, a dog and its bone, a job gone, money and love missed, then we lose our way so quickly. Some of it we can never get back.

Without the supernatural, humans are just bones. Everything is more remarkable than me at all points and times. On the river, I felt my irrelevance every minute. Nothing is smaller but only larger in knowledge, space, and size. My wisdom is acquired, received by sharing, and sometimes even stolen for advantage. Human emotions, the urges we have, decisions we make, what we want and do, and those things we do not wish for or don't want to do are the unwisdom of humans, human-made and human-planned things. I am traveling on the river for just what I want. It is not bad, but according to Solomon, *everything is meaningless.* The truth is real, whether that one in us or that of a mystery.

A need to control with only helplessness to do it, all more significant than me, than any human, yet creatures of mammal, fish, insect, or bird are better at accepting this than we do. When we don't recognize this, we live a fantasy and some unbelief, or maybe a frivolous lie here and there to feel better, while other life does know it and lives it as its truth naturally. No animal life pretends to know everything while having vast abilities to rule the world, except for humans.

CHAPTER 8

Signs

The waters were high and flooded over banks on both sides, and the current was steady but not as swift as the day before. I had just left Swimming Bear, a lone paddler's campsite, where I slept well and long enough. The camp was notably raised above water level, almost fifteen feet. I hoped it was dry up top even though it was difficult to reach when I arrived at dusk. After tying off to a large scrub near a spread of water weeds upstream from the site, I walked through the marshy access and up a narrow slope with my gear.

It took four trips to maneuver a thin strip of hard ground that plunged off to the right, down a high crag of mud, and into the center of a fallen tree submerged in moving water. Opposite that drop, to the left of the path, was a dark thicket of brush, brambles, and twisted young trees that rolled down a boggy slope into a dark hole. It was a rich tangle filled with extra-large mosquitos hanging in the air and darkness like a fairy tale. If I went into it, I knew I would not get out.

I was unsure which would be worse, the thicket and mosquitos or the mud-torn edge with the half-drowned tree. The roots of the old-growth tree lost grip, let go into flood water, and tore down the face of the riverbank as it keeled over. It made a lethal strainer with no one close enough to hear my cries if I got trapped, so I preferred the dark undergrowth if I lost my balance. I leaned toward the brush to steady myself but was sometimes forced to walk sideways with my back toward the thicket when washed-out sections tapered the narrowed footpath. Fortunately, I stayed upright with my gear bags for balance, like walking a tightrope over a pit of hissing, riled snakes.

Despite its challenging entrance at low light, I found the camp flat and dry. I saw a fire ring with blackened wood, old food wrappers, a picnic table, and a small grassy portion that perfectly fit my shelter. Otherwise, it was surrounded by thick forest and an overgrown trail that unrolled back to a small hunting blind hidden in the trees. The structure faced the marsh below, where my boat was tethered for the night.

I set up my tent but zipped it to thwart mosquitos, then leaned on a tree overlooking the ever-moving water below and the channel from where I had just kayaked. There was complete silence now that the river had slowed for the night. It was hard to comprehend that this was the same Mississippi River I had lived near most of my life and many miles south. After paddling on it for hours, I loved seeing it from above while settling for the night. There was a sense of conclusion and satisfaction in those moments against the tree, like finishing a book's last pages. A fellow boater and his teenage son were paddling about a day behind me, so I wondered if they might draw up nearby at any moment. But nothing.

The river stream was crooked as a serpent for miles before Swimming Bear and after. Tree growth was thick along every meander and the inner banks. The shaded light was green and evenly dim, and the air was a quiet contrast to the dramatic, threatening water throughout my day. I went to bed without a meal because I was tired and got under my quilt for a deep, peaceful sleep. The night was without visitors of any species or imagination.

After coffee, dried fruit, and a protein bar for breakfast, I broke camp, reversed the tightwire act, and went down-river. The day was a surprise as the flooding worsened and picked up pace after continuous snowmelt flowed from the headwaters. In some wild places, rising waters moved fast and obliterated the Mississippi's channel. One thing was no longer set apart from another. Forest and pasture lands became indistinguishable from the river, becoming a giant's lake. Boomerang-shaped ponds, previously formed along the river from up north to Louisiana, called logans or oxbows, should catch and hold the overflow. But they were obliterated and no longer helpful.

The river, streams, oxbows, and woodland trees all looked the same, one large sea swirling in circular patterns every-where it spread. Water moved every which way, crisscrossing currents and swift flooding channels. It wove over and under the river's more sensible course, triggering a sinking feeling that I was about to get lost.

Surreal was the only word that described this day. It hap-pened forever and countless times in those backwoods river bottoms, but who was ever there as a witness? The turmoil was commonplace for the water and forests, but I read no human testimony. Complex and laborious for a kayak paddler, I expected one thing and got another instead. For all that, it was still the wilderness. How many eyes had ever seen it and then made plans to civilize it, adding rest stops, directional indicators, or warning signs? It's just not the place for this change to happen. Before this day, I saw extra effort put into warning or directing a lost traveler in only two locations.

Days earlier, I paddled slowly downriver and enjoyed the calmness when I came to a fork not marked on any map. The one ahead and another to the right was a larger open water span, crowded by trees and river growth that peered above high water. The space was circular but choppy at the edges, almost as if dug out by hand and deliberately made crooked, with two sizable homes on slightly rising banks. It looked like an overfilled sink with a sucking drain pulling and swallowing pressured water. In the center of the large pool was a stand of old trees surrounded by floating patio furniture and leisure equipment peeping up from the waterline. I saw the top of a large barbecue grill, parts of two lounge chairs, some soggy chair cushions adrift, and what could have been the legs of a trampoline, but I was unsure. I sat at the juncture, paddling in place, and wondered which route was the natural river and why that furniture was floating there.

To the sharp left was a widened river stream, calmer but moving and with less complicated details than the option to the right. A jon boat stood on end against a tree in the distance. Evidence of heavy flooding, I knew, and someone's boat had come to rest vertically against a tree. They had no vessel to recover it because they needed their boat to retrieve their boat. That is why it was left, I assumed. The underside was blue and white but saw better days, now paint-chipped and scarred.

Neither left nor right, but at the crotch of my crossroads were several trees downed by beavers, their toothy evidence scattered around stumps left above the waterline. Fresh wood scraps and flakes were remnants of recent activity, so I knew the beavers were nearby, maybe watching me wonder which way to go. Like the flooding, beavers came and did their damage, then acted innocent the next day.

The blue boat had floated free from its mooring, and furniture was lost and unclaimed. Beavers and water worked overtime, then left a pile of trouble. And now, where was everybody? It was silent and deserted, but for water trickling quickly in tight trails down the opening to my right. The ground in the bowl was lower than the riverbed, so it drew in river water with loud, continuous swigs. I could have easily flowed down in and crossed the littered expanse. But looking to my left, it seemed the more obvious choice, so I turned. That water was calmer after it drained off its pressure into the junk-filled bowl as it vanished behind me.

I passed the vertical boat and followed an apparent right turn. Along the upstream side was a smooth-as-glass stone-wall that rose gradually as I followed its base. It felt like a rising canyon, but only on the northbound side. At its top were some rustic homes or cabins, some occupied, and others seemed abandoned. Ahead was another turn, this one to the right but with small flooded islands and a house straightaway, before the turn began. I discovered I was hovering over a flooded pasture near a farmer's barnyard when I drifted toward one island. I quickly jerked right and continued where I thought I ought to go.

As I paddled, I went through some floating objects, a lawn chair, and a grill, and then I saw trampoline legs again. I realized I was in the water-filled basin but from its backside. I had just circled an oversized, indiscernible island made tall with white pine and ragged stone outcroppings across from the canyonlike wall. Like a secret plan against me, the flood waters had drawn me around the rocky mass and down to the low basin, where water continued to pour from all sides.

I thought it looked easy enough, so I paddled toward the beaver trees across the side. It was only a slight slope rising and going out, but the flow shoved me back, streaming in more potent than it appeared. I could not get out, even when paddling rapidly and firmly. I was trapped in place, like going up a down-escalator, so I moved over and tried again—the same. Again and again, the result was unchanged. I saw no people but knew I was not alone there. I remembered the beavers were everywhere. But neither beaver nor human rushed out to assist.

The pressure pushed me away, but I knew all sides of the hollow rushed water toward me, and I was weaker than its strong push. After an hour of struggling, moving place to place around the edges like a clock hand, I located a less pressured stream. Its descent was gentle as it curled around beaver stumps and poured over thick forest grass. The underlying factors worked in my favor to weaken the flow and ease the incline. It seemed the perfect place to maneuver around the water jets that opposed me. I backed several yards and paddled swiftly to rush the calmer grasses. Once there, I grabbed the logs like handrails and slid my way inch-by-inch until the bow of my kayak grabbed the momentum of the main river, and there, I was released.

The blue boat was ahead again, so I veered closer. That is when I saw it. A worn rope was tied to the tree, intentionally holding the boat in place, and barely visible spray paint said *Mississippi River That Way*—a right arrow pointing toward the high stone wall and farm at the end of the channel. I had traveled in this direction before and had gotten nowhere, but I was relieved a human had marked the trail. Now, at least I knew this much.

I returned to the farmer's pasture and dropped anchor two feet to cowpie-covered grass. I rested there while studying maps and my GPS locator. Even though the basin's farmhouse, barnyard, fields, and playground were not marked as river, I only saw this one expansive lake that made no sense. So I rested and ate a granola bar.

To the left, ahead and behind a heavy treeline that bordered the farmer's front yard, I saw a river emerge from this enormous reservoir of chaotic water. I thought it must be the Mississippi River, so I pulled anchor and crept cautiously to the left, jabbing my paddle down into the underwater grass to stay on course.

The pull back to the sink was stronger to my right, and I was concerned I would need to fight it again. As it climbed, I rose with the land underneath and portside as the water overspilled what looked like a tractor draw from one pasture to another. As I paddled across its front lawn, the farmhouse was now to my left. A broken barbed fence was posted between two trees where a lip of something horizontal made a defined ridge. The river water hurried toward it, falling into the next section like the sheet of a six-inch waterfall.

As before, I could not manage any traction to overpower the flow. I didn't know how safe it was over the shallow drop or what might come after. I kept my eyes on the grassy bottom near the surface as I watched it alongside my kayak. Even though the force of the water was pushing me out, I tied my boat to a low limb of a tree as I passed it. When I felt secure, I raised from the cockpit, placed my feet on the soggy grass below two feet of water, and braced against the current.

Grabbing the bowline, I untied my kayak, pulled it slowly like a wagon, and stepped cautiously toward the siphon. The current was rushing toward me and away as I walked in cross-current at the surface and undertow below. It pulled like mayhem beneath, but fortunately, I could place my steps deliberately until I reached the miniature spillway. I discovered the ridge was made from a fallen fencepost stretched between its wire, creating an outflow into the flooded riverbanks. When my bow was ready to go over, I grabbed hold of a crooked fencepost and jumped into the cockpit. At that, I let the water force take me in my kayak as it discharged into the Mississippi River channel and adjusted my pace and tempo to match its own. Afterward, my day went smoothly, thanks to a jon boat directional placed in my path.

A less dramatic and shorter circumstance with a warning sign occurred downriver but above a lock and dam. I was not lost in this one, although the sign I encountered stole my day's peaceful, relaxed journey. The river was quiet, serene, and easy to trail, so I enjoyed it.

Out of nowhere, a small concrete building appeared on the raised left bank at the river's edge. As I got closer, its definitions were more explicit. There were no windows, a flat roof with a large overhang, cement stairs with a maroon pipe rail that went to a solid steel door, obviously secured, and no one in sight. To the left was a graveled pad grown through with fresh Canada thistle, likely a place for a service truck or a worker's car that rarely came. Tall weeds and grasses grew thick around the other sides of the smooth exterior walls. It was maybe five hundred square feet and completely unmarked. It was creepy but interesting, popping up from nothing in an isolated place.

When I got closer, I saw a large sign facing the river, almost shouting a warning like this: *SUDDEN UNDER-WATER DISCHARGE, DANGEROUS TURBULANCE! STAY BACK!* The narrowness of the river made me question where to stay back, so I slowed my speed and weighed my options. Mechanicals and technology inside the building must initiate the sudden forceful discharge when no human can predict it. But a person did paint the warning using a broad brush and black paint on a white-colored rectangular board.

These could be cooling waters, I imagined, from a nuclear plant or city runoff through its drainage system. Even though I was a lone paddler, innocent enough, the technology and pipework could not know or care that I was passing just outside. A hundred feet were between me and where I should be to avoid the pandemonium from sudden forceful turbulence in the river below me. An image flashed of my kayak balanced dangerously on a whale's airstream rising high over its blowhole. I backed up, set my paddle, and raced like a panicky squirrel crossing a busy road.

Safely outside the discharge area, as I crossed its invisible boundary, I slowed to continue my path down the river, feeling glad no whale had surfaced. Another channel converged with mine not far downstream, and near it was a second hand-painted sign. Again, black wide-brushed letters on a whiteboard, but this time, threatening anyone who gets too close would contend with the sheriff. Eighteen hyperboloid cooling towers were set on the opposite bank in two daunting rows along the river. This was a swift and startling change from the forested and nature-filled river I had paddled for hours. An enormous nuclear plant sprawled out behind to the west. An oversized pool of cooling water sat near the river edge, pouring used water down a release chute into the southbound river. The puzzle made more sense, and I was grateful for the instructional signs. Stay away from the power plant, cooling towers, and under-river discharge, or you'll be in trouble with the sheriff. Easy enough.

CHAPTER 9

Grasses

During the morning I left my night camp, the water suddenly began to show intersections, like paved streets, going to the right, then the left, and ahead to a three-legged corner where a stop sign is expected on a surface road, or at least a blinking light or yield sign. The waterways were more expansive than the riverbed below and, of course, not paved like an asphalt road, but heavy with thick water just as dark. I monitored my GPS in real-time but needed clarification because each turn only appeared correct. The directionals were scattered, and nothing was as it seemed. I turned wrongly into a channel that ended at a right turn only, then an impasse full of soggy trees, so I made an about-turn going back.

I paddled ahead again and saw a smaller track through trees with options to go right or straight into a wider channel. I took it and followed the right. Water swirled, and I had no choice as it pushed me again toward another right turn, this one sooner than the original on this same main course, but it was a mistake. When I emerged from that route, it was near a tree cluster, exactly like I saw before, because it was the same one. I knew I had passed there earlier, maybe twice or more. Then I heard myself say, *look what you've done now* as if blaming me was going to help anything.

I repeated my way forward but chose different ways every time. Each way led right back to the same tree bunch. On the last pass, I veered over the edge above a submerged riverbank and aimed with the purpose of a striking arrow right into the trees. I grabbed a tree trunk, spun my boat slowly until I faced outward, and then leaned against one of them to rest myself. When I left my refuge, I was no more relaxed with no better idea than when I'd arrived.

It was getting late, and I needed to resolve my predicament or risk sleeping upright in my kayak all night. The fears about that idea were unspeakable, but be assured, they were about snakes, bats, and spiders or falling asleep and tipping out, which made me shudder. I imagined how dark it would be at two a.m. on this inky water with me alone. I refused to even consider it and went on looking for a way out.

More hours passed with little progress, then the worst thing happened. My phone screen went blank, preventing prompts, calls for help, volume or brightness changes, and GPS images to examine my problem. My most essential tool was utterly disabled, while my wearable GPS indicated the screen as active. But it still would not respond. I needed navigation because, with it, things were much better, I pretended, even if I was still lost. Because being lost with navigation was better than being lost without it.

I was confused and exhausted by the loss of options as the

day shortened. Continual GPS allowed me to stay proximate to the river channel, even if moving over submerged banks and wooded ground. This was how it went all that day— slow, precarious, and no progress. Later, when it no longer mattered, I learned that overuse of the navigation screen and humidity inside the watertight pouch could cause it to overheat and shut down for protection. This was for the device's safety, not mine, and its timing was awful anyway.

Being lost at some time or another is part of living. Lost on the road or in a new town, attempting to fix trouble or adjusting to a complicated situation, lost in a book, or not paying attention. At times, we get lost in ourselves. Reality is gone or how we know it to be, and we cannot identify what should come next, like in a flooded river. While we're lost, the worst is when we cannot help ourselves. Any solution is beyond how we think or what we can do. It seems impossible, disturbing, and challenging to ask for help.

*   *   *

At any moment, I can replay a vivid memory of being lost, as real as that day, an impossible and unsolvable situation. These memories stay lodged in our core, ever-available to call on. Even at eleven years old, life experiences were weaving into the fabric of my being, so feeling lost felt the same as it did now. My sister took a Sunday afternoon babysitting job during my fifth-grade year. At the last moment, she changed her mind and did not want to go, so she persuaded me to do it instead. Of course, as the compliant and willing younger sister, I agreed to it.

When the man pulled into the driveway, I did not recognize him as a regular babysitting customer, but I left with him anyway. I thought he looked too young to be a dad and was scruffy with dirty hair. I had not known a grownup man who was this unfriendly or impolite and kept a cigarette hanging off his lip for the whole car ride. He did not speak to me, but I knew exactly where we were going as we went across town. So I was not afraid.

The street was fifth avenue east, the main one I took to school at the west ward building, and to get to the fairgrounds or my grandma's house across the highway in the first block of fifth avenue west. Across from my school was a blue house belonging to some twice-removed relatives, and the babysitting man lived at the corner of the highway and fourth avenue west. I had no reason to be afraid, and I wasn't because I knew how to get home. It all was familiar.

I recognized most of the houses in my town, except for the babysitting house. I had never noticed it, kitty corner of my school and across the road. It had lost all its paint and was weathered-gray with broken wood steps sinking into the dirt. The house looked like a garage on the outside, but it was a shack. People lived in it. However, I'd never been in one before, but I might have seen something like it on television. Before we went inside, the man told me his wife was at work as a lounge singer. He wanted to see a ball game at a bar on the highway. That's why I would be watching his kids, *so thanks for doing it,* he said. I didn't say anything back to him, and we went inside. The man immediately turned around and was gone before I learned what to do or his children's names.

The floors were rough wood, old, bare, and dirty, like a shed. The couch sat where someone dropped it after they carried it inside, crooked and in the middle of the room. It faced a cluttered countertop across a space that seemed like their kitchen. There was a dirty stove with a broken door, a refrigerator with rounded corners, and a finger-marked edge. Its handle was sitting on the nearby counter. I did not see a table or chairs, nothing like that.

The shack had no stairs, just the three rooms on the main floor. The couch room, the kitchen area, and a bedroom. I could see them all from the one spot where I stood. The only space separated by an open door was the bedroom, but I could see an unmade saggy bed and see-thru curtains that hung long to the floor at both windows. This place felt like a cowboy hangout, but nothing I had noticed in town before.

Young children were everywhere, but they got quiet when the man came and quickly went. I counted six, all dirtier than the dad, no one had shoes, and then I realized he had left them alone when he came to get me. The six faces were smudgy, their hands were grimy, and all were towheaded, hair sticking upright like they never had a brush. I saw no bathroom, maybe why no one was clean, and the youngest two wore wet, droopy diapers. I didn't notice where to get water because I was not there long enough.

After the man left me in charge, the children stared at me. I stared back. Only a little older than the oldest boy but the one responsible, I knew I needed to figure out how to fix everything. First, I should wash them up, comb their hair, make some good food, find the toys, and go outside to play. I did this at home with my young brothers and sister and other babysitting families—first, the food, then take care of things, then play, all of us. I always played when I cared for children, until I grew up.

I went to the fridge, but it was empty, except for beer bottles. There were no cupboards above, only one below that was jammed with cereal and cracker boxes and a mouse trap. There were no milk jugs or soup cans to match the cupboard food. I had not learned how to make food without all the pieces and directions. So I didn't know what to do.

Before I could make a plan for everything, the six children began to scream and holler. Some cried, and others played rough, but they all went into motion, jumping on the couch, knocking each other every which way. I tried to calm them to make some order, but my voice could not penetrate the commotion. To them, it seemed I was just another kid to ignore.

Thinking back, being lost on the river, unable to find a way out, felt like the day at the shack. I was in over my head with severe consequences, no phone back then, and my lost GPS on the river. A sense of helplessness grew quite suddenly in both. But I have never known how to give up on the impossible.

The afternoon barely began when the children's shouting and disobedience worsened. My despair snowballed. I felt I was not a good babysitter and could not stand up to this job. My hope diminished, and I realized how deep in I was, unable to resolve this and lost in every way. I backed into the third room, sank onto the loose bed, put my face in my hands, and sobbed. A few moments later, the house was quiet, and I heard a small voice. *Look, she's crying,* it said. The oldest child had calmed the room, and all six had circled me.

I don't know what happened or how we left after that. But all six children were standing in a line on the sidewalk, me in front, as we started walking northbound in single file toward fifth avenue. At the corner, we crossed and turned west. My grandma stood at her front screen door watching, holding the door as we approached. *I saw you coming,* she said, and we filed inside. *I need help,* I said and started crying as she pulled me close as always, and then she made sandwiches and milk for seven tender-age children.

My grandma suffered from lifelong poverty but was rich in heart and had an even bigger kitchen table. As we ate, I heard her say to no one, *I hate seeing babies go hungry.* It was all I needed that day, her ever-loving kindness and the feeling of being found.

This is proof that humans do not have answers for everything. We can become lost more than we can prevent it. A sense of lost and truly being lost brings the same thing to anyone. There is no difference in the emotion of either. Utterly lost, then utterly found, there is nothing like it. Neil Diamond sang that *being lost is worth the being found.* He was right.

I have rarely been lost, but I recognized the familiar apprehension on the river. I was lost in the center of nowhere, unable to set foot on dry land. It was a lostness bigger than I could imagine. I had lived it at the shack and other times after that, knowing no one and nobody to call or find me, no coffee shop on a corner to wait, and no hotel to rest or delay until my route was clear. This was an unnatural, eerie, and adventuresome experience that most humans want to avoid.

It might have been less dreadful if there had been sun and the clouds were not hanging so low, but they were limp just over my head. Thunder rolled through them, intimidating like a threatening dog's growl. Who could know how it would go, so ominous and menacing? I loved finding my way across flooded waters and to my grandma's doorway that old Sunday.

Lost after Swimming Bear was like other days before. No dry land was in sight for hours, and all moving water masqueraded as true river. I came around bends I had already circled. Fallen trees converted to familiar landmarks after I thought I'd paddled for many linear miles. I feared the worst. I could not imagine what would come from the deep, dark nighttime in this swampy, water-logged place.

I headed toward a tree in the middle of a channel, put my arm out like before, and hugged it. My boat stopped as if I had slammed the brakes of a car. I sat there, raging water all around. I prayed for some help long ago, but now, hanging onto a tree, I yelled, *I am calling OUT!* I felt an idea come over me right then. *Look down,* I thought. There they were, three inches under the water's surface. They had been there all along. Grasses. A large patch of long river grasses, an elementary lesson for any paddler, *grass points the way.*

Distinctly, underwater grass, magnified by clarity. Every blade pointed behind me as they fluttered in the rushing water. Grabbing my paddle, I let go of the tree and made turn-around strokes to follow the grass as it flapped underwater, like long hair in the wind. No matter gust direction, flood course, surface speed, water depth, or overheated technology. Below, the natural current of the Mississippi River was surging like it always did. The grasses continued to point in unison with that flow, turning to exact points at every curve.

Floodwater and surface grasses only mimic the river but are found out as they flutter willy-nilly every which way. But actual river current grasses point true, all the same, then turn gently as the river curves around land, rocks, and trees, even if the land is underwater. I followed the grass for five miles and ended up at a raised campground just before dark, a dry campsite ten feet above the river and just sized enough for me.

I have not been lost from the disorientation of time and space or was ever left unfound. I have survived, yet just barely at times. Unlike animals who follow simple instincts again and again, humans must think and make choices differently in each situation, with too much worry or a sizable conviction. Only one is possible at a time. One obliterates the other, whatever we decide. Self-reliance is a choice or the more extraordinary spirit of nature, air and space, energy, empowerment, and possibility. Things that are bigger than humans, wiser than I have ever been, only one can be chosen logically because both do not work together. Not ever, believe it or not, it is a law of nature or gravity, of spirit, a rule of how things go, naturally and mysteriously, something we cannot tamper with even if we wanted. After my fear, some worry, and autonomy, I saw river grasses.

We are not more significant than this grassy compass and no better than honey bee instinct or homing pigeon's route. As sap slowly rises, then quickly boils to sugar, branches in the wind, and tenderness of vines blowing, we are not greater. Hang onto the fundamental roots of anything, and there will be the truth. As if honey bees or homing pigeons brought me in, but no, it was not them. It was the grasses. Fear is like a charlatan, a snake in the woodpile that gets you while you work. But here, instead, the grasses' natural bearing and orientation were hopeful, trustworthy, and unfailing, with no deception or impersonator nearby, but as if they had magnetized points.

It was not even me who did it, but a supernatural compass, trusted, down any street or on a river.

CHAPTER 10

Old Man

On a day in July, while kayaking sixty miles above St. Anthony Falls, I had in mind to paddle south until I reached secluded parkland to the west of the main channel. It was named clearly on my river map. Only a few patchy unreserved campsites were available, one for me, my modest personal things, and kayak gear. The place looked like good timing to call it a day.

As I moved nearer, the riverbank was thick with woodland and undershrub but no perceptible break with a ramp or take-out. I thought I must be close to the approach, so I hugged the shore and paddled with a measured stroke to avoid a miss. I favored this day's water with the swift current because it accelerated my strokes through noonday. But now, I needed to maneuver my brake on speed to make the quickened turn when it appeared.

Well, things went differently than planned despite my forethought. With the combined swiftness of the current and abrupt arrival at the ramp, I needed to rapidly swing out to make a direct ninety-degree turn and then slam onto the gravel incline to get enough bow landbound. Setting ashore this way was necessary to prevent the water's forceful flow from taking my boat at the stern and towing me backward downriver at a swift clip. This water had muscle, and I feared I could not bear up against it if I did not prepare.

In seconds, my landing could happen just as planned, except when I looked up, plain as day, I saw a thin-skinned old man. Someone parked him there, I determined, after he moaned too many days about getting out fishing. This is how I saw it at the time, in that very instant.

The man was at least ninety years old, wearing a spent tweed ivy cap and a dark blue anorak zipped to the neck on this warm day. His bare ankles shined like snow in sun as they separated his too-short twill work pants from his tiny stretchy socks that stuck out of his hardened black shoes. Whoever set him there had unfolded a card table chair and placed it squarely on the gravelly boat ramp. This is where the man sat with chin to his chest, holding a fish pole, sleeping.

I must have made a noise when I anticipated what would happen because he raised his head, smiled, and said, *Oh, hi!* as if he had not seen another human all day. His face was gaunt but simultaneously soft, and I imagined he was malnourished under his old clothes. I disguised my alarm with a smile and shouted *hi* to him but quickly yanked my paddle to straighten southbound again as if I had no intention of jamming up on his ramp. If I hit this fragile man, life would never be the same for either of us from that second.

Losing my campsite was a small price for the old man and

me dodging the consequences of a collision. As the strong drift propelled me downriver past the entire length of public camps, I had no regrets. I conceded that it was still on the early side of four and a good chance to practice my locating skills for a random island campsite.

The DNR supplied sites upriver from where I had come and were welcomed when things worked out. But some of those camps were atop unreachable banks or blocked by leafless fallen trees intermingled like a game of pick-up sticks. Others were mud-flooded and brimmed over with dime-sized mosquitos beyond any human endurance. This was all blamed on spring season floodwater. But the river was now preparing for change as levels were lethargically receding and random island or riverbank camp possibilities gradually emerged. This is how it would go from here down if I were lucky.

Miles had passed when I saw a cluster of small islands with a larger one toward the rear, all situated along a subtle kink in the river. Their ground was covered in green, appearing soft and inviting for a night's perfect sleep. I would need to pull between the smaller ones through a draw of fast-moving water as it split from the river and compressed into this narrowed swell.

Using my held-back maneuver from the old man situation, pulling outward then jerking landward, my bow would slide right up on the island as I had meant but abandoned earlier. It happened as intended this time, but the land was extraordinarily muddy and even soupy after recent flooding when these islands were underwater for a significant time.

What appeared as a thick pad of grasses was sparse and flaccid, like it could come undone any minute. I rose from my boat anyway to walk around this one and give it a test. Much too boggy for a tent, I decided, as I sunk ankle-deep into the smooth, shiny slop as cold ribbony strips oozed back through my toes. I glanced back at the second island and noticed a tent-sized mound in its center, visibly dry as it rose above the flood plain. It was at least eighty feet across the diagonal channel, but I thought I could do it.

First, I planned, then got in my boat and said lightly over the river's roar, *I need help to do this.* My mind was set on a dry, secure camp for a good rest, so I knew I would have to paddle nonstop and full speed at a descending forty-five degrees to cross the channel and land high on the dry part. I was sure to make it if I did not break paddling for even a microsecond but kept squarely head-on.

It started as strategized, solid and forceful, swift paddle strokes keeping me straight on course. But then it happened. Just seconds in, I unexpectedly glanced to my right as if on a dare from someone. This eyeblink triggered more hesitated strokes and immediately caused my freeze-up. I knew what was happening right as it came. I was locked in position and could not react. It was clear I needed to get back to it, but I did not put my stroke right as the water's rush took over. This tick of a second was all that was needed for the powerful down-bound to take advantage. Until then, we were evenly matched with my determined and quickened pulls, eyes locked on the bull's eye, and the water with a mind of its own. Everything was in slow motion now, and I knew this letup lost it for me.

Rather than crossing the narrow channel, the current shoved my boat sidewards, like a plow ramming snow, into the middle of a fallen tree. I was snagged inside the center branches, a deadly strainer, as the water shoved with fierceness from behind. The tree limbs bounced me back like a series of springy coils. Any way the force took me, I was absolutely snared. Like a black fly in a sticky web, the spidery limb above held me in place. Despite all that was happening, I still believed I could overcome it.

With a click, my position changed. The kayak was now pressed on the water parallel to the tree's main trunk, bobbling powerfully along the backwash. From a spiderlike grip inside the strainer to this swaying giant of a tree trunk, I finally felt the uncertainty of my overconfidence.

The boat was suctioned to the pounding log, not letting loose even as I pressed with both hands to move forward along its length. As the water shoved hard against my kayak, I was lifted and tipped sideways by what seemed like spiny fingers curled up from the underside and determined to dump me out. The last thing I heard was my moaning voice, *Noo! Nooo!* The grotesque silence of underwater followed, and I thought I would die.

While I hung inverted in the Mississippi River, dangling head-down from the cockpit, I saw the underside of the water surface three feet above me. It appeared like an outline of black ink from a fine-point drawing pen. The water was the color of lucid tea, brimming skyward. The underside of the surface had a thin waviness like windblown sand dunes. The transparency made it impossible to know if this was water up there or air waiting for me to take it. The delicate details of that moment looked like a fine watercolor wash. Then, I realized that I could not rise above the turbulent undertow.

A kayaker's most perilous wrong, I had placed a small

unsealed dry bag near my feet, low in the cockpit. It had filled with water during the overturn and become stuck as cork. I was trapped firmly in place, unable to escape my cockpit seat. My body rounded up toward air when my flotation device strained to pull me to the surface, a confusing struggle against gravity, but with no result. Words of disbelief were audible in my mind. *Is this really how I'm going to die?*

I knew I had only a moment left, and hardly that, as I imagined the first lungful of river water rushing in. Split seconds passed as a rebound abruptly winched my head toward the air. I felt it, cool and breezy on my face. I wheezed and pulled in a sizable breath before sinking back into darkness. It was a divine inhale, a size to last, but I wondered, *for how long?* I had foreboding dreams of this during winter when working out the hazards of my trip. But I did not want to accept it playing out like this now.

As I used up the big gasp, I realized I had been unknowingly kicking loose from deep inside the cockpit. When my feet let loose, my body became weightless like cottonwood seed drifting in the wind. My PFD behaved as designed and lifted me confidently against the gravitational force. I felt cool air wash over in seconds as if it was waiting patiently for me up top. The eerie silence ended when I surfaced into the rush of booming water. I was suddenly slammed into the side of my bottom-up kayak, still lodged against the bouncing log. There was no time to think out my next move. The water surged against my boat and flattened me along its slick hull. Unable to grab on, it rapidly forced me across as I slipped the entire fifteen-foot length of it and was spewed into the downstream surge.

Still attached to my marooned boat were my paddle, a paddle float, a rescue strap, and a bilge pump. This safety gear was useless where it was securely fastened. I was tumbling like a ping-pong ball while gulping and spurting a mix of water and air. I felt unsure how this would play out as I watched my gear shoot past me down the narrows. I do not know what made this next thing happen, but it was indeed redeeming. My hand reached for a clump of grasses at the last curved tip of the island as I careened by. I slammed to a halt as if I had hit my brakes.

Clinging to it with all my leftover strength, I knew my life depended on my tight grip. The power of the water's rush continued swirling around my body without sympathy, but the wild tossing had propitiously come to a halt. At least it seemed over for the time it was.

The orange bag that plugged the cockpit was aimed at me now, coming fast like a shot. As it hurtled closer across the water rush, thoughts of its crucial contents ran through my mind. A floating flashlight, waterproof matches, two space blankets, an extra battery pack fully charged, my old sweatshirt, one protein bar, a full water bottle, and my best-loved rainproof trail jacket with hood and reflective trim. Everything was packaged in dry bags inside for just this type of calamity, which, despite being prepared, I did not expect any of it.

As the bag careened by, I lunged to grab it. But it was swollen with water and fully weighted like a bowling ball. I could barely bring it in. I fought to hang on to the mud bank but was pulled backward by the bag's deadweight. Still clutching the grass clump with one hand, I wrestled the bag with the other, then tossed my knee underneath to push it up top. I had placed it wrongly and was almost killed for the mistake. This was a human blunder, and my overconfidence that did it.

There I was, after hanging upturned in swarthy water, now dangling off a grassy clump with roots loosened in sucking mud. I was breathless, dazed, and exhausted but still alive. All this might have taken six or seven minutes from start to end. Then it hit me, I needed my phone, or I would hang on this grass wad like a pendulum in slipstream all night or longer.

At the start of my day, I jammed a charged battery pack in plastic and lodged it under my PFD shoulder with my cell phone attached. Now its cord flailed like a loaded fishline extending into the sudsy water. The phone might be connected still but may have taken in water since I had removed its waterproof case earlier. I walked my fingers swiftly along the cord, hoping to find the phone at its end. There it was. Barely plugged but still attached, bobbing hard in river foam. I snatched it and dialed 911 quickly.

When I heard a voice saying, *what is your emergency*, I felt frantic to tell my full-length story in the first seconds, but no matter what I said, the operator could not hear me. Through a water-filled phone, I could only listen to the dispatcher, both desperate to exchange a message. I shouted above the water sound, and she yelled back, still unable to hear.

After trying for what seemed too long, I remembered my waterproof satellite beacon, also attached to my PFD. It was still fastened and fully charged right where I had put it. I grabbed it, flicked the rubber cap, and pushed the red SOS button. Nothing. It was supposed to be instantaneous, but on the second try, still nothing. As I nervously turned it over to read the tiny directions, I realized my glasses were gone, so I could see only an inky blur. Breathing more rapidly, I pushed the button again, pressing for more seconds. I heard the emergency sequence chirp as the colored lights raced around the device in an urgency algorithm.

Only moments later, I listened to the same operator speaking with an emergency response coordination center in Texas. They connected local first responders to those needing help through satellite emergency devices like the one I carried. They were in trauma mode, preparing a search-and-rescue effort on my behalf. A jolting relief poured over me with an intensity I had not felt before. Help was on the way after my solo attempt had failed out there near nightfall.

It felt slightly familiar to me now, this clumsy struggle followed by a bumbling of my own rescue. The dispatcher called me that moment, insisting I pull out of the river. *Can you get on land? Are you able to get out!* she shouted. *You MUST get out of the water! Can you hear the sirens yet?* I suddenly realized how intensely cold I felt.

I clung to the sludgy embankment of the same mud island I had initially tromped across when seeking a camp. My ill-fated diversion toward dry ground had left me shoeless, sightless, helpless, drenched, boatless, and right back where I began. All my gear was underwater, if not floating somewhere downriver by itself. My hair had pasted to my forehead, trickling dirty water through my eyes and down my cheeks to my mouth. Mud was everywhere it should not be, and I wondered if I would ever come clean from this.

Mixed in, I felt the driblets of sadness and embarrassment for my failures of that day. It was not the first time excessive surefooted self-reliance had taken me down, but it was likely the worst ever. I knew this time I had brushed close against death. My mind flashed an image from the farm years before.

Willie was my yellow puppy, only months old and still soft, with big feet and ears like mud flaps on a truck. I wanted her to feel comfortable near large farm animals, for this was where her life would be. That day, a grown horse was grazing on barnyard weeds, so I placed Willie in grass nearby. Nothing happened at first. The draft horse nonchalantly crunched on stems and waved its long tail against flies. My neighbor's horse was staying short-range in my barn but accustomed to its own dogs at home across the road. Willie teetered unevenly in the thick grass, going off-balance before catching herself and getting nearer to the horse.

The broodmare's right rear foot raised out of the blue to catch Willie and fling her high into the air. The horse's large eye glared sideways at me, teeth still chewing. It was indeed no accident but cleverly quick. I ran across the barnyard to Willie, where she landed gasping and terrified, just like me in the river. It was my failure there, too, trying to teach the pup too soon about comfort with big creatures. My goal was her self-assuredness as she lived out her future there, but she nearly died on day one. After that, she never would get close to livestock bigger than herself.

On that same farm, I raised my child's training wheels too soon, even though they peddled fast on their bike across our lawn, and didn't even tip over. They just rode more quickly while yelling back, *you can let go now!* Even though I had already released many meters before. Years later, they were good at the bike and in technical college at fourteen. *Is this pushing beyond really that important,* I questioned, as I lay spent on the island point waiting for help.

Pulling enough on the grass to peer over the edge, I saw a slippery rock planted in the mud. My fingertips clung to it as I pulled myself onto the riverside using strength I did not know I had. Laying across the muddy bank, I heard the dispatcher still calling to me. *I am out, yes, I am on the bank!* I shouted through my phone, which had shed enough water to be usable. Now that safety was closing in, I realized the efforts I had initiated for emergency responders and the worry of my family, who was notified back home. But I knew it was either this or I could die out here, freezing to death in the night. This is how it happened exactly.

Some moments passed when I heard the sirens and eventually spotted rescuers descending a steep ridge slope on the westward shoreline. Four white shirts and arm movement went through dense brush hundreds of meters beyond. I saw the brush tops and scrub trees shaking as if a pride of lions was passing underneath. The rescue party hand-signaled at the water's edge to confirm sight and hold visual contact from that distant outer bank.

Two hours passed before a rescue scow approached from a downstream launch point four miles below. It raced around my island and abruptly slid to the muddy top beside me. Ostensibly, within seconds, I was inside the lifeboat, wrapped in a blanket by a three-deputy team. My kayak was extricated and tied to its stern before we sped downstream. Back at their departure point were fifteen more rescue personnel waiting in line to hand me off one-by-one until reaching dry land, near the readied ambulance and sheriff's deputy. It was an extraordinary force performing a lifesaving mission for me, this all-volunteer squad on a late Sunday near sundown.

After being verified unscathed and expressing my gratitude, I was driven to a local hotel. At the same time, rescuers transported my boat and gear to the firehouse, where it was stored until my family arrived the next day.

That next dawn, my feet hurt so badly that I raised my pant legs to discover swollen ankle joints. They were ringed in dark blue and reddish purple bruises, resembling wide plastic ankle bracelets. Here was my reminder and proof of how hard I kicked to escape my underwater trap, where I had a foot in the grave and an incredible day of survival.

From my real-life paddling trip, the fragile old man and I were made safe for another day on this back-breaking and mighty river. The moon of that night must have been the two survivor moon.

CHAPTER 11

Weather and the Wind

Most of us do not live unhoused or without shelter, and fortunately, we do not endure changing weather all day. On my river trip, I lived outdoors but had adequate refuge in a light-duty tent away from rain or sun. My kayak was partially protected from river water, miry weeds, and tall grasses when I used its cockpit skirt and cover. A yellow jacket with a brimmed hood repelled other rain when it came.

Like rainfall, the heat could be brutal and difficult to avoid, but it wasn't persistent. I was guarded against it by shade, my hat, and heat-protective clothing. Some days were not exceedingly hot, but others were sizzling and humid. I went without shoes on warm days and dipped my feet overboard to cool. It was not unpleasant or cold during this summer's paddling trip, but when chilly and damp, I had the equipment to cope and outstanding sleep gear that self-adjusted to temperature fluxes.

Elements of the natural world are generally sporadic but

within our power to mitigate. It is usually not perpetually hot or cold and not continually rainy. In most places, it is unusual to see constant rain, even if genuinely wished for or needed by a fretful farmer. What makes us feel most frantic is the tenacity of any persistent thing, whether rain, fog, wind, or temperature. Our peace of mind is affected when we cannot pause or change it.

Chinese water torture was designed to torment people with endless drips to their foreheads. It wasn't the water, drips, or forehead that caused the peril but the constancy that couldn't be stopped. What we are forced to experience for prolonged intervals profoundly disturbs our human psyche.

During my kayak trip, I paddled for hours on some days and spent significant time alone while camped on shore. My mind meandered through memories and other life adventures or repeatedly assessed daily weather. Only wind was constant, in one way or another, but other weather features were ever-changing. Wind worked well with temperature to remediate the heat, even in unpredictable shifts. But rain and heat did not show the same randomness as wind. We are naturally reactive to the unreliable nature of weather, like a temperamental, erratic friend. And wind is like that person switching from one mercurial mood to another through a single day.

*   *   *

I had an adventure with an unrelenting weather disturbance after I left O'Hare Airport for New York City. It was sunny in Chicago and again at LaGuardia. When I boarded my five-hour flight to Heathrow, I wanted clear weather to continue, but it was raining heavily when I landed. After several drizzly days in London, I flew to Schiphol Airport to wander Wassenaar dunes and tulip fields in Holland on foot and by bicycle. It did not take long before the heavy rains of England followed me, so there were no prospects to roam anywhere. I left Amsterdam by train for Belgium, where cats and dogs were raining there, too, so I was forced to eventually continue to Germany, where an acquaintance met me at the depot.

I settled for several days in the northeastern corner of Westphalia, where the pastor in Minden was my host. As he drove to the Rathert family farm, we went over winding country lanes through the now so-common downpour. Soggy pastures were separated from the road by low fieldstone walls that rolled for miles and had endured the test of history. These dry stone barriers confined grazing flocks of white-headed mutton sheep drenched by rain. They were a prominent German breed known for fruitfulness and their ability to withstand damp weather, perfect for this gloomy day.

On my family farm in Wisconsin, our sheep were similar but a smaller breed that produced lean meat and triplet lambs, sometimes twice a year. When pregnant, some ewe mom's bellies reach near the ground. Their sturdy resistance to wet and cold weather helped them adapt to the upper river valley where I lived, and they ordinarily nosed through deep snow for old field grass. I felt pleasure and comfort far from home while traveling over the German countryside and watching familiar sheep forage in the rain.

The pastor unexpectedly slowed his vehicle and pulled to a roadside jetty. He placed his right arm over the back of the driver's seat and turned to look at me. A few seconds passed, silently staring at one another, when he finally said, *we are sorry what happened in the war. We want you to know how sorry.* He was born after the war. That was forty years past, but he carried the remorse anyway. He turned back and continued driving toward our destination. This was not the last time sheep and war coincided in my story.

Because it was storming, my cousin Heinrich, the local postmaster, and the extended family played strings and sang folksongs while we ate indoors. Days later, I boarded a train to catch a boat on the downbound Rhine River. It was raining, so I could barely detect Rhineland castles or nearby shorelines through the thick, hazy showers. By now, the sound of relentless bombarding rain pelts was distracting and unsettling to my peace of mind.

I arrived in Heidelberg for a break, but navigating the small, water-filled streets was an effort. The roads were empty. Everyone was inside during the vast and prolonged rainstorm that followed me across the UK and Europe. I carried my baggage up a slope and scanned all directions for my lodging. A man stood in the gloomy light at the corner ahead, arm raised, motioning me toward him. Weighted with my backpack and a day bag on a wheelie, I turned to walk his way, but he walked further and around a corner. I reached that first corner and turned as he did, but I could no longer see him.

Further ahead, the same man stood on another block with his arm raised and hand signaling. I trudged toward him without thought for my safety because of the tedious wet weather. Again, he disappeared around a corner, bordered by tall sculpted hedges dripping with rainwater. Hesitant to turn onto another deserted street but eager to reach the inn, I risked it. Like last time, the man had paused ahead, arm raised and motioning back and forth with his finger pointed across the street.

I glanced to my right and saw my lodge, an old-world building of worn reddish-brown brick, four stories and taller than it was wide. Several small sashes divided by tiny panes of thick bubbled glass lined the façade. An amber glow from a room indoors revealed the corrugation of the aged window surfaces.

Monochrome human forms floated inside like shadows. A row of patrons was along a dark bar, some with elbows leaning on its rail. Most figures wore hats of various sorts, probably to dodge the rain. Musical notes floated through the damp night and were coming from the tavern. The view was overly inviting as I stood outside watching from the rain. But I knew I would not fit in, a stranger and a woman loaded with luggage, unable to speak the language. Still, I was eager for a warm shower and dry clothes, so I started toward the door, where a sign directed me toward check-in. As I opened the painted red door, I glanced back to signal thanks to the stranger, but he had already vanished.

I spent time in the narrow guesthouse above the bar on this tight, constricted street. The rain endured, and my expected coziness at the inn was disrupted by constant punishing thumps dropping hard on my windows, the roof, and everything.

When I finally left Heidelberg, I headed to Switzerland and longed for dry warmth and sun. I was only presuming it would be good weather because rain over all of Europe for my entire stay was altogether improbable. But I found Switzerland no different. In defiance, I took a small boat across Lake

Lucerne to Mount Rigi and around the edges of a glassy blue lake beneath the Alps. Despite the rains, my visit was incredible, beautiful, and pure.

The rain had disregarded my hardships and continued to pour wherever I went. I was grateful when the evening arrived that I boarded a train to Paris, where I rested the entire eight-hour trip in my sleeper car. It was a private, quiet little space with a red-plaid woolen blanket and down bedding over my bunk. From my window, I watched people running with umbrellas to escape the downpour as they rushed through the night to board at dark stations. By morning, my train slowed into Gare du Lyon, a bustling rail station where I ran through the rain to catch a taxi to my hotel.

The real-life rain in Paris was not romantic like Caillebotte portrayed in his bright *Paris Street Rainy Day* canvas when he painted it with oils in 1877. Years before, I stared at this piece in Chicago and wondered about the romance of a wet Paris. But now, as I sought refuge in my room, it was dull gray and drab with the relentless, oppressive drizzle.

Days passed until I left for home on a long flight to New York, where I finally escaped the rain and was pleased to land on a dry, sunny afternoon. The experience of sun warmth and crisp, shiny air was extraordinary after weeks of damp clothes, wet shoes, and monotony. Ever-present rain blunted my senses and banged on human nerves, but even so, the journey is carved deeply into my memory.

We have been given a medley of natural differences for good reason. Despite thriving in stability, humans prefer the essential variations of the earth. The faithfulness of European rain has not jaded me, but almost.

* * *

Taking to the river in my kayak brought a welcomed assortment in nearly every way, except for the wind. It became my ever-present and reliable warden, no different from overseas rain. It never abandoned or mollified me or gave any relief from itself in any way. I was acutely aware of the perpetual nature of the wind and became familiar with its many forms and styles. This was new to me since wind is frequently overlooked and unseen by most of us. It is often trivialized, even when it's endless, because we have shelter for cover. Paddling so many miles alone gave me too much time to contemplate this relentless wind.

* * *

On some farm mornings drenched with dew and peaceful air, we sat on the back porch under clear skies, wondering where the wind was. As time passed and dew evaporated, we watched clouds form above. Delicate cirrus grew out of plain nothing and reminded me of cotton candy swirling inside a pan, turning bits of sugar into fluff. The cirrus swelled into cumulus by noon without us aware it happened. Like a puffball mushroom bursting with spores, the clouds filled with dew drops until they nearly ruptured.

Each day we were there, one of us would say, *here comes the wind,* and sure enough, it came. On those cool and early mornings, dampness rose until the wind appeared on our high ridge, often forcing us into the house. We planned farm chores around the winds because they picked up quickly and were strong. At that time, I saw the wind as a farm inconvenience, but now I know it was physics more than annoyance, and it happened without my input.

Science explains that wind is a movement of large amounts of air, mesmerizing and bewildering. It surrounds us, whether awake or asleep, conscious or not. It continues without us knowing or assisting, just like the spirit and energy over the universe we cannot see, and many humans do not know at all.

Science-placed accounts about wind leave us still wondering, *what is the origin of wind?* Humans cannot grasp the probability of anything that has no beginning but has existed forever. Now, before now, and after now. It is incomprehensible and perplexing to our limited wisdom regardless of how things get explained. Ethereal movement and energy, gases, and things unseen and mighty are mystifying, and none of it ever sleeps. I heard the wind whistling just last night when everyone was sleeping. It is mind-blowing.

*   *   *

The same wind showed itself during my paddle through a daylong wetland in the headwaters. It matched the expansive size of the marsh, and its moving air followed the water trail that switched all day like a snake tightly looped and thirty miles long. I enjoyed it entirely and was, for a part of it, led by two loons as they plunged under and surfaced later up ahead. They went more than a hundred meters submerged and, one time, popped up within feet of a third loon that had been swimming alone. All three vocalized loudly at each other as if discussing how loons travel in pairs, not threes.

Finally, the newcomer loon paddled off and submerged separately. It stayed close to the first two but respected their distance as a committed pair. The original loons reset their pace and continued leading me through. The two traveled together, but like me, the third continued solo and disappeared, maybe offended or hurt by the earlier rejection.

An odor passed through the headwind out of nowhere. It was fresh, intense cigar smoke. I paddled all day without seeing a human, but this was undeniably a person-initiated aroma. The dried cattails and marsh grasses extended in every direction and seemed miles with no solid ground to stand upon. But the cigar scent was unmistakable and did not linger once it breezed through, obvious and steady as it went.

I became more watchful for others after paddling in a relaxed and inattentive mood, not feeling the need to beware. I grabbed my rearview mirror attached to my boat by a thin cable and scanned behind shoulder-to-shoulder. I saw nothing and no one but what I already traveled in the expansive marsh, miles ahead and the same behind. No land anywhere to walk, sit, or stand.

I traveled three more river miles when I saw a jon boat ahead, sitting idle and crossways in the river with several fishlines cast. It was still too far for details, but as I approached, the profile of an angler appeared. He wore a saggy fishing hat and oversized jacket over his hunkered shoulders. A large cigar dangled from his mouth, and its smoke curled before it breezed off. I slowed as I passed and told him, *I smelled your cigar way back.* He apologized. *The only way to smoke without upsetting the wife,* he said. I smiled and told him I enjoyed the surprise of it, cigar on wind in the wild. We wished each other well, and I moved on. The wind brings humans together even when we are apart, and it continues whether or not we like it.

*   *   *

There are many ways to experience and describe wind, to

learn what is in it or how it is made. Physics, meteorology, climatology, philosophy, and spirituality or meditation have been used. But who knows the mind of wind? It is an esoteric momentum and energy, a felt spirit that is unfathomable and revered. Enigmatic. Invisible but still known, completely indestructible, yet it can crush and demolish at will. Humans know better than to hook wind like a fish or bottle it like water.

Dams hold back water, but no structure holds back the self-reliant wind. It blows through walls and under a roof, making windows rattle and trees whistle. Of humans and wind, the stronger is wind, a reason wind is feared by us and seen as ominous. Wind can drive an alfalfa stem through the bark of a walnut tree as if it has intellect greater than ours. We can't say that wind has no soul when it picks up a person and then drops them somewhere else. The wind is out of human hands.

I have seen windmills draw up water from the earth. But when the wind comes too fast, the stop-lever is pulled to save the blades from tearing in the too-strong wind. Civilizations built shelters for many reasons, but the highest one was to protect people from wind. I still love the wind anyway. When humans or babies do not come to life, we blow wind into their lungs to wake them. Wind is life. It brings alive our spirit to join with spirit. Wind is a spirit so robust and unshakable, of its own accord, moving or not moving things on impulse. Is it science? Or is it a state of mind with a soul and essence?

The wind is the determinant additive to anything that otherwise would cause less damage alone. Floodwater can overflow everywhere but remain smooth and flat until the wind is added, like lowering a high-speed mixer to a cake. It becomes multiplied in fierceness and power. Have clouds, and add wind to equal a tornado that swirls dirt and houses together. Wind was liable for moving the 1930s Dust Bowl that darkened skies over the American plains. Undoubtedly, the wind added to human decisions that set up devastating conditions.

Newly devised deep-plowing machinery removed grasses that held topsoil to open ground. Native prairie grasses with deep moisture-seeking roots and prolonged survival were yanked out and tilled under. Clump grasses that held tight naturally, fountain and feather grasses with wind-defiant tallness, were sacrificed for this new farming. Unforeseen drought loosened the now-unstable topsoil and naturally turned it to powdery dust. This chain link caused the settlers to collapse into poverty, illness, and starvation. Hundreds of pioneers were stricken, made vulnerable, and laid low. The government did not know what to do. So it did nothing. The dust bowl was formed and became a perfect set-up for what came next.

The wind came to stir dust into clouds called Black Blizzard Storms over the entire high plains and low, from Canada to Texas. The wind was not held back by anything, no prairie grass, roots, forests or terrain, buildings, towns, nothing. It had free run across the plains and prairie where it lifted millions of micro-dust particles, thick as cement, blocking daylight and making air unbreathable. Barns and houses were filled with dust so high that animals and people were plugged in or out and could see only a meter or two ahead. Brooms and dusting cloths no longer worked on the dust, so shovels were needed to move it, but there was nowhere left to pile it. Respiratory disease was unchecked, crops died from dust cover, and livestock starved to death. Water was nowhere, but if found, it was undrinkable and thick like a slurry.

The wind moved the dust into everything - nostrils and shoes, horse manes and children's ears, bedding and dishes, eyes, lungs, and mouths. Even cow udders stopped producing milk, and dust-buried chickens no longer gave eggs. Food was contaminated, and wagon wheels couldn't turn. One of the worst windstorms carried dust clouds across the plains as far as Chicago, where records swear that twelve million pounds of dust layer was left.

The wind made the skies dark across mid-America, even on sunny days. Without it, the devastation wouldn't have been so bad. The wind moved the dust until the day was black, the air was rigid, living things were buried, and life suffocated.

The same wind, a monster blowing dust into nimbuses, was outside my camp right then. Sleeping in a three-pound nylon tent, pinned to the ground with six stakes and four guy cords, brought wind to my door. I rested with my arms folded under my head, waiting. What was the wind up to out there? It had never whipped itself up to lift my tent or tear its door off, but I knew it could and once almost did.

The sometimes-deadly wind, friendly when warm, clattered like a rattlesnake to let me know it was out there. It made me humbled and bothered. I needed to admit wind was supreme, and I was not. I bowed my head, then went to sleep soundly while the wind stirred up something but whistled nonchalantly. My tent nylon, waterproofed polyurethane, kept me a width of twenty deniers, with one denier the width of a silk strand, apart from the wind. A thickness I could push my breath through if I felt like trying. Yet even then, I loved this wind.

*　　*　　*

One day, I walked three miles, hoping for a breeze. It came abruptly behind a stone wall or randomly from trees in a row, then left. I wanted more than was doled out, but I had no say. As I walked, I thought about how invisible the wind was, how we know it by feeling, or how it caused things to happen. It does so much without a motor or fuel, wheels or sails, and no help from people or animals.

During nights at the farm, we knew the northern wind by a steady steel flap against steel, a loosened corner of the barn roof striking on itself. Southern winds came, too, making a separate drum from sheets on the opposite face just as high up. Stormy times made music up there when both ends wagged all night, composing plain tunes and rhythms that kept us awake till the gusts passed us, and we could finally rest.

The wind is many things to humans. It brings water to the surface and power to our homes. Wind carries things, crashes other things, and scares us. It snaps and breaks old trees. It can also freshen the stuffy and blow stink off our clothes after winter. As we now know, it takes tiny dot-sized flecks of top-soil and balls it up to make a deadly dust bowl.

*　　*　　*

Our farmhouse was built by a man's hands in 1865, just like the barn, and his ax swipes are still seen on the attic beams and hay mow. They are big and rock-solid against the wind, so we could miss a storm when it came over our place. We saw chickens and farm elements flying longways through the yard and across our window view on a summer day. It was the only way we knew a storm was out there. There was no shaking or rattling, no vibration of any sort, but a neighbor's house shattered, and a trailer upturned in a field with the resident who was napping but now stood stupefied in the rubble.

Wind did not hurt us or clatter the place but harmed the others nearby. The old builder must have known what it would take and how that wind did, but we never know until it ends. This wind makes things wear down and break apart, all done suddenly or slowly. It can be for the good or not, but how do we know while it is still moving.

On Sunday, the sheep flocks knew to run and secure their place in the barns before we shut the doors. Their noise signaled something, but only they knew what it was. So we packed up and drove to a distant town to buy a breeding ram for these ewes. That day was sunny and pleasant when we started. But turning for home with the new ram in the truck, the radio alerted us to stop and not go north. It said, *a tornado showed on radar.*

We changed course, but the alerts kept coming for the roads ahead. We zigzagged our way across Iowa with the bleating ram and a young child in the truck's backseat. The winds chased us, and we ran, turning everywhere as if hunted by a pack of sneaky wolves hungry for breakfast. We outran the danger and made it home all right, but the tornadoes beat us there, wrecking roofs and houses along the way. Humans are at the wind's mercy and sometimes made to feel foolish.

* * *

I spent my working years in Chicago, nicknamed the Windy City. Much dispute about this, whether the windy nickname came from an old politician who talked too much, or the city rested next to a great lake where the wind pours off. It swirls around tall buildings, through the Loop, then spins and eddies down subway tunnels. It could be both, but I know about this wind as a longtime resident.

Driving after work, I saw a woman blown over by the wind. Her fingertips touched the ground near her toes, intricately balancing not to fall. The strength of the wind kept her teetering this way. Her long skirt blew up and over her head, blinding her face. While the fierce lake wind held her, nobody rushing home could find a place to stop. I found a way to pull over and draw her into my car from a grassy edge. She was already elderly. Already homeless and, by now, alone. The wind did this to her anyway. She had no fightback, no one to call, and nowhere to go. I wondered why this was put upon her and not on me or someone else.

After Lake Shore Drive, she only wanted food and to leave my car. She directed me to a large, empty house with a heavy concrete porch covered with people. She tried to keep her food private, she said. Inside were others who welcomed her but did not warm up to me. I still question why I didn't take in more meals. Forty years passed, and a profound wind and a hungry old woman still stuck in my mind.

*   *   *

So many stories about the wind, but wind did not end my traveling adventure while on the river. Although it was with me continuously like a pesky companion. On day one, I did not notice the light breeze that was so calm and pleasant. On day two, I paddled against heavy wind through a large, long lake where the wind made itself home. The brutal waves slapped me and pushed against my progress for hours. By day's end, I was diminished after being whittled into a smaller shape by the wind's sharp and rowdy energy.

Heat and cold, rain, darkness, velocity of water, not one of these a leader like wind. Each day's gauge began with a wind assessment. From what direction, how fierce, is it twisting or straight-on? Is it gentle and light? A friendly or cold-hearted wind today? Is it low at the surface or over the trees? Will it raise the water to bind me and my boat? Wind's nature is critical overall as it makes rain into bullets of lead on skin or the air so thick and hot to breathe. During a flood, wind moved the water quickly and fitfully, causing me to call for help. Twice.

During midday on the expansive Winnibigoshish, the wind has raised water in seconds to several feet by blowing forty mph over a twelve-mile fetch. Lake Pepin is sometimes worse despite its half-size to Winnie. With twenty-mile ridges, Wisconsin east and Minnesota west, the lake bottom is two miles wide. The wind is known there at Pepin for its intensity across the width and against the bluff walls.

The Coast Guard reported the rescue of paddlers all summer, including me, who could not reach land, took on water from high windblown waves, as I did, or lost navigation when the wind would not let go. Again, me. Lake Winnibigoshish is famous for waves that come rapidly and so close together that there is no time to take cover. This is how it is with the wind out there.

These are stories of wind, invisible but moving the visible, to let us know it's there. It is incredible to be unseen and still have power to move a house or lake of water, bring down an age-old tree or break a roof, mess up our hair, blow off a hat, or cool a sweaty face. Wind will not be warned or told when to come or where to go.

It will make a cyclone or blow a little puff, whatever it feels like doing. Asking it to stop will frustrate anyone because the wind blows on its own. It whistles, but its sound is only against something else since it has no noise. It comes winding around a corner or through limbs of tall trees, taking dust to Chicago to show off its clout, bold as brass, quivering panes and doors, pushing back my loaded kayak, slamming me sideways on the river, splashing water, and threatening my tent flaps. Once, it drew the air out of my lungs like a vacuum sucking up floor dust. The wind is mysterious when we are told tomorrow's breeze is northern, and then it comes due south as we wake at sunrise. The wind puts a stop to my boat and then makes it go.

Spirit is wind, and wind as spirit. God is spirit. Humans are spirit. Pure, valued, and blessed. Compatible but cautious as we go our ways, we are never quite sure because we think we are different, but we are not. We are the same, only lesser. Once all is said, the wind gives us our vitality, and we don't provide it with anything. It has motility as it moves on its own, pushing lungs in and out, making nostrils flare, and creating a wave of air as we cross a room.

We can have it in our sails, close the window to it, let it flap our clothes on a line, or put up a break so it will not douse a fire. Whether circling the drain, floating a boat, tossing darts, flying a plane, or bobbing in an ocean, it is the physics behind the air movement of wind, a kinematic motion, strong like a locomotive, and its spirit. It wants us out of its way, a mind of its own. I have learned much from my ubiquitous, infinite, and not always tender friend, wind.

CHAPTER 12

Locking

Lock-and-dam facilities favor locking all vessels in priority order. Still, if various factors or conditions cause a considerable challenge to the ranking, it is the lockmaster's decision to shuffle and reorder passing watercraft. Of course, military boats and U.S. mail carriers are at the top of the status list but are often unseen on our inland waterways. Next are commercial passenger boats, then commercial tows - the barge industry and for-profit fishing vessels - and recreational boats with an order of importance all their own. Larger cruisers and private fishing boats may be instructed to clump together in the lock chamber, and a lone kayaker is advised to wait as a matter of safety or logistics.

Sometimes, a kayaker is led to the front of the line while motorized recreational boats are held behind in the box. This allows the paddler to exit without the backwash of others or in the trail of propellers and speed. Other smaller but motored boats, like jon boats, houseboats, and pontoons, can go through in a mix as directed. The lock operator decides how it goes, and that is final.

After realizing I was paddling toward a lock first thing one morning, I used my marine radio to connect to the lockmaster and ask about thru-passage. If I arrived before a specific time, I could get right through, *no problem,* he said, because no priority barge or boat traffic was coming from either direction. This news contributed to making good time for my morning ride. I packed up, put my boat in the water, and began the three-mile trek to the locks, current and wind in my favor.

When I arrived, I again radioed the lockmaster to inform him I was there. *Plans have changed,* he said. *Please make yourself comfortable,* his nonchalant voice sounded through the static. A series of tows went through a southern lock and continued toward this lock-and-dam. Despite the invitation to come earlier, the operator decided to gear up for the priority arrivals from downriver at the lower facility. As a result, he rearranged me and my kayak in the queue.

Although the barge tows had not even arrived at the south locks, this prudent lockmaster prepared the lock chamber for the coming rush. Despite my reasonable forethought, I was told to delay for three hours after sunrise. Instructed by the lock personnel, I should line up along the eastern shore covered with riprap and no means to exit off the river. Three hours, time enough for all tow fleets to lock below and then move north the twelve miles to lock through where I was obligingly waiting. Just an estimate, these three hours could take longer if any tows needed splitting to get through either or both locks, doubling or quadrupling the time until my lock-through.

A standard lock capacity holds fifteen barges at once, three abreast and five long, but not all have the same. Only the lockmaster knew the inside information about what was coming, and his best guess was my three-hour wait. *Could it be longer,* I asked. Out of the gravelly transistor, he said *it sure could. Tows could be coming northbound or more from the south. Who knows,* came his relaxed voice. Being anchored to rock for an uncertain three hours would be a challenge. Without the ability to leave my kayak and go ashore, I knew I would take on the wake of every passing tow and motorized boat, pushing me into shoreline stone or turning into every roller as they came. Likely, I'd be paddling in place like this for half the day when I'd prefer to put my paddle to better use and make some miles.

Meanwhile, any tows coming southbound would need to wait for those northbound. The queue would be juggled again, pushing me to the back and causing me to wait all day. By then, late afternoon anglers would be looking for a bucket of lunkers or at least gunning their motors first at the favored fishing holes. As for me, I'd be tossed like a sock in the washer. It just did not make sense for me to wait.

I didn't know what was downriver directly after this dam. If a good island camp or sandbar followed the lock exit, I might wait to get through by sunset and have a place to set up camp before dark. Not knowing made it a gamble I did not want to take, so I paddled back upriver, where I launched earlier that morning. Current and wind were against me, doubling my time returning upstream to my starting point. When I arrived, I found land transport for my boat, gear, and me and was dropped at the dam's far side. I paddled into the twelve river miles, watching those backed-up tows slog past me as I traveled south.

Good camping may have been likely, but my lesson was learned. Locks are public passageways at no cost to boaters, but the preference for trade on most rivers surpasses any mutual movement. Inconsequential paddling boats like mine are not revered even though they are willingly locked through. The priority order is a fixed condition for traffic flow through hundreds of worldwide lock systems.

Only one category of floatable vessels lies below the kayak or canoe class and is not allowed to lock through. That is sit-on-tops, stand-up paddle boards, a river raft of logs and rope, inner tubes, or a rare homemade barrel-and-boards without rudder or motorized propulsion, except a paddle. All these are at the mercy of the current, and passengers sit or stand on, not in, the vessels. These uncomplicated and plain objects are deemed clumsy and unsafe, so are banned by these strict rules enforced by lock tenders throughout the lock-and-dam system. The phrase, *easy as falling off a log,* did not come out of nowhere regarding safety on the river.

To further disappoint, little or no help is available, and few paths are prepared for portaging around locks and dams. Approaching the locks on top of an unacceptable vessel means only one thing – no locking available. Even though I had the proper vehicle and correct equipment, I could not lock through before a long wait, so you never know what will happen. It is just beneficial to be prepared for anything.

*   *   *

Most people haven't paddled through river locks but may have traveled on a locking tourist boat into bigger waters while vacationing. When in Amsterdam, I wanted to go to the North Sea. I arranged for it, then eagerly arrived on time for the boat. At once, I fell asleep and stayed that way the entire length of the North Sea trip, never viewing the sea itself or the canal that took me out there. At the time, I could not say whether there was a lock-through at the mouth of the sea because I was not awake to observe it, but I presumed there was a large and busy one.

Later, I discovered a lock facility at the North Sea Canal that differed from our Mississippi River lock-and-dam designs but had the same intent and operations. Even though I slept through the cruise and have no recollection of locking through, it has lodged in my memory of something I have done.

Other touring locations have locking facilities, like the Soo Locks at Mackinaw City, one of the world's most hectic water transport systems with permanently heavy traffic. The Chicago Harbor Lock that sits just off the shore of Lake Michigan at East Lower Wacker and Lake Shore Drive is also ever busy. Tourist boats and commercial crafts lock back and forth at the harbor, where there is little room to conform to the varied heights of the river.

Many commuters take the subway under the Chicago River, but others drive over the lift bridges that connect downtown traffic. When river traffic requests passage after locking, bridge tenders drop street barricades and elevate the bridges skyward, halting traffic entering or exiting the city center. All twenty-nine movable bridges remain high until boat traffic passes, underscoring the priority set on the river. This is the necessity of water traffic, whether business or leisure, slow going through a major city or any rural farmland when showing its order of importance.

When I passed my hometown while paddling the Mississippi River, Sister Karen Neuser, who followed my river trip online, asked about my locking-through experience. She wondered, *was it difficult, scary, or just what?* I admitted I was uneasy the first time, not about the water, the large chamber box, or other boats. But that I needed to use the correct language through my marine radio to request locking caused my nervousness. It is essential to connect with lock-keepers to remain on task and in line with their instructions and safety expectations.

When I initially called them over the radio, the lockmaster did not respond, which caused me to worry. I wondered, *did I forget to say 'over?'* I pushed the radio button again and said, *over*, then added *roger* for extra measure. Maybe I was heard the first time, but they did not answer. Did they listen to me and answer, but I did not hear? Or did my message reach no one? I continued my doubt and concern. Was my radio broken? Or was it theirs? While bobbing on the water eight hundred feet out, I ruminated over these questions until I heard a voice come back with basic instructions buried in static. *Wait ten minutes while the chamber is prepared. Watch for the green light*, it said. Green light? I did not see any green light.

I was tempted to paddle closer, another hundred feet maybe, but what if a barge tow was inside and came jetting out when the gates opened? This was probable, I thought, but maybe not. Barges don't jet at any speed, and the mitered gates open slowly before a barge moves out, traveling sluggishly

heavy. Still, I was concerned, but not yet frantic, about everything possible, whether plausible or not. I cautiously worried
as I became acquainted with the routine. A worse and more
logical problem could be a draft of barges coming silently
from behind while I couldn't hear it. One would be my deep
focus upfront on lock details. I could only spin so many
mental plates at once, and was already busy and preoccupied.

Years ago, at the air and water show on Chicago's North
Avenue beach, I rested on a blanket, staring through the trees
while I waited for the event to begin. I thought I was dreaming when I saw a large black shape float slowly over the foliage
above me and low enough that I saw its creases. The movement was barely visible as it drifted across like a heavy ghost.
However, I knew it was real and not a UFO on this special day
when the entire city was on the lakefront. It was not until it
entirely passed and the tail crossed over that I heard its angry
thunder.

This was the Stealth Bomber with all its sound sacking out
the rear. Barges are just like this. Their only motorized noise
discharges from the tail of the tug, pushing way back from its
silent approach, leaving the engine blare for last. Even more
challenging, the tow pilot cannot see over the frontmost edge
of the barges, mainly when they are three or more deep, flat
lengths lightly weighted and raised from the water surface.
This is when a kayaker is left in jeopardy and must know what
is underway at their front and rear.

While waiting for the lock approach, I repeatedly held up
my rearview mirror to be assured I was alone in that water
space. Bobbing while stirring my paddle in place, I held steady
and acted blasé as I watched intently for the green light.

Rabbits do this, appearing relaxed in grass but with all senses alert. They don't want to be caught in lethal circumstances any more than I do. I did not answer Sister Karen fully then, but I hope I have by now. This was my experience, tense and tiring but thrilling all at once.

From half a mile out, it is not easy to recognize the direction or layout of the dam and its associated lock. Ellen McDonah, a well-known and accomplished river paddler, met with me when I camped nearby. While at the river's edge that day, she told me that *distance flattens and distorts like a mirage*, which confirmed our shared experience. *The dam itself is the most important to get correct*, she said while we sat just south of home. She described her experiences as I envisioned mine, both mindful of the river and our memories kayaking over it. This was a rest day at camp when Ellen visited. The warmth was from the sun and our time together that afternoon. The complexity of locking, which direction a dam runs, what side the chamber rests, and our reflections of paddling alone were all in our shared thoughts.

When structures were first noticed ahead, I used a laser monocular rangefinder. It was easier to isolate the lock location, single-handedly using its one-finger focus wheel and holding steady on the paddle with my other hand. This was essential because studying the locking chamber area took significant concentration. I looked for these things straightaway: a motionless tugboat on the landside and a small, green-roofed building - the lockmaster's structure or the visitors' deck - because either one marked the correct side for entry. As Ellen said, *the last thing a paddler wants is to misjudge any of this.* They could paddle up to what appears to be the chamber, only to find it the dam itself. There would be no recovery from a mistake like that, and the thought of being sucked through the dam rollers is horrifying.

Our local paper recently reported that human remains were found in the Mississippi River sloughs just south of town. It said the body belonged to a man who appeared to be in the water for a long time, and its condition suggested that it passed through an upriver dam. It is essential to know what is ahead, how it is laid out, and which way to pass through. The man may have just been out for an evening of calm fishing but lost his bearings.

After identifying the lock location, I looked for two large yellow patches on each side of the chamber's opening. A massive wall always followed one of the patches, which was the route to the interior of the enormous lock chamber. The green-roofed structures and this giant wall were always on the same side. With all these identifiers found through my scope, I looked for the light with my naked eye.

A blinking red, like a roadside stoplight, is standard lock equipment. But the view of it was intermittently obstructed because the fixture is set to a tug captain's level, raised high on the water. The position of the light has not been considered for a paddler's low level on the water, which is only a couple of feet off the river's surface, yet we needed to see the light just the same. As I rocked and swayed, the light came and went behind parts of the lock chamber and the moored tug. If I blinked, I would lose it from my sightline entirely. It is this light, when seen, that makes the whole system work like the period at the end of a sentence. If I paddled up on red, I would risk being drawn into the gates' suction as they pressed open against the pressure. But I would not see my go-cue if I missed the green while bobbling like a floating seagull at six hundred feet. This could annoy the lock operator who prepared the lock for me, but I was absent from the queue.

Missing the green go-light would also cause an intense and rapid paddle for me to catch up to the process that had just begun without me. Paddling hundreds of feet to reach the entrance wall, then continuing along the lengthy interior to the inner chamber, and finally paddling behind the lockmaster, who casually walks the upper wall to where I should settle, takes enormous sustained energy. Most paddlers would want to be ready when the red light turns green.

Once inside the chamber, I was typically led to the last five feet just before the downstream gate, which is closed when facing it. I felt uneasy close to these gates but knew this placement was intentional for my safety. One unexplained purpose that a paddler is moved to the front like this is to create distance from the wake of the motored watercraft at the rear. A tail vessel must idle slowly at a considerable distance even after being released from the lock. If a paddler had to fight the wake of any boat, plus the severe turbulence directly outside the gate caused by the discharge of chamber water, these moments could become problematic and require frantic paddling to reach a safer downstream current. I have been in the vast lock chamber alone on many of my lock-throughs, but it was a controlled and respectful situation when I was with others.

These details are mostly always the same as I describe them. It was as though I was going through the identical locks repeatedly. The experience was just this much the same each time. Except once, as I sat in my boat holding the rope end lowered to me, the lock employee shouted to me while trying to overcome the noise intensity. He told me that he did not want to offend, but it would help, he yelled, *if you could speak louder into your radio when calling for a lock request.* I shouted back. *I appreciate the advice because I want to do what works best.* But most of my reply was reassuring him that I was not offended by his suggestion. At the same time, he hollered back that *most people are bothered when corrected.* When I called, *that's okay,* he could only shout *WHAT,* very loudly. Even when it was difficult to hear one another, I believe our sentiments were exchanged adequately. Locking through, but especially working at the locks, is full of noise pollution and possible dangers to a person's hearing.

I know that manners and respect for the lock workers are essential. The workers need appreciation for doing a repetitious job, in heat and cold or rain and sun. They must be meticulous about boaters' safety, and sometimes for customers who are not grateful or ever satisfied.

The lock man told me, at the top of his voice, that he works many weeks uninterrupted but then takes consecutive weeks off as well. He thundered *YES* when I hollered back, *do you like it that way?* It seemed like a monotonous job and one he mostly did alone, possibly lonely, on the river doing repetitive actions. So, hollering or not, he seemed to enjoy our conversation. I thanked him with a wave as I paddled out the massive beveled gates following a tiring encounter for us both.

Another encounter with a lock was at dam eight Genoa when the hundred-year gates were replaced. A notice was sent up and down the river that this lock would close, specific dates and hours, to accommodate pulling out the old gates to make way for equally massive new gates. The job was mind-boggling and complex, and I was thankful I did not have to do it. I locked through just as the gate change was completed.

I felt privileged to see the century-old wooden gates that had spent decades below water, finally set against a crane awaiting a barge to haul them away somewhere else. The new gates, magnificent and painted steel blue, were still without a scuff, only days since installation. In another hundred years, they will continue to hang there, making the same motion repeatedly with no complaint, but I will be gone. These new gates moved quietly and smoothly against the pressure of so much water. I could barely shout loud enough for this lock-master to hear, *do you notice a difference?* He yelled back, *sure do!* These new gates were the once-in-a-lifetime experience that gave me an unforgettable day on the river.

All people in any approved vessel can go through the locks while respecting basic rules, good manners, and aware-ness of the lock operators' efforts to protect everyone. It is routine and unforgettable, a worthwhile, memorable, and nerve-racking adventure.

CHAPTER 13

Lock Gates

It is an old and constantly active river. Early in the day, I arrived at my secluded island, and boat traffic kept me from feeling listless. Several dozen pelicans meandered on a nearby sandbar disconnected from my camp. Mayflies used me for a perch, and a few king-sized fish quickly rose and curved back underwater, making a loud slap. I felt the startle and some anxious reluctance about carp slapping me in my kayak when I continued downriver in a couple of days. Eagles moved smoothly overhead but kept going on their hunt for food. They knew better than to grab at a carp.

A thirty-barge tow slogged heavy on its way through, right in front of me, where I sat in the sand only two feet off the river edge. I watched it round two turns downstream, do the straightaway in front, and then another turn to the upbound side to finish my view of it. Its wake rolled in slowly but forcefully against the shore, sounding like a big dog lapping too much from an oversized water bowl. The splash made my feet wet as I sat too close, but it felt cold and refreshing. Soon after came a single colossal tow that looked like a seafaring ship. I didn't know where it was going and could not think of its inland purpose for pushing upriver. My wondering eased as it passed in near silence since its business was none of mine. I had just come ashore to make camp when this traffic went by.

I eventually unfolded my camp chair in anticipation of more promenade and was not disappointed. About seven tows lumbered through while I waited for dusk. When I glanced upstream this last time, a single-barge tow appeared at the downbound turn from the north, heading into the pin-straight section in front of me. I observed with acute interest because this one was conspicuous. I could not decipher its tallness and odd-looking cargo. As it advanced, I thought it was a small apartment building set upright on a barge. It was marked by unusual stature for someone riding on this quivering river. The architectural form was repetitive, as if rows of windows were outlined by beams going two or three stories high, like any ordinary landlocked building.

The tow went slowly, progressively angling to make the sharp bends without tipping. This distorted its depth of field and left me even more puzzled. I could have reached for my scope to get a better look but felt too lazy, so I waited until it passed closer. I realized how wrong I was as it finally paraded by my quiet and peaceful island, me groggy from the sun.

This was no maritime vessel from another part of the world. Nor was it a merchant's fancy apartment on a water cruise. These were the four massive chamber gates removed from the Genoa locks upriver earlier in the summer. As I locked through there, I saw them next to a barge hoist, waiting to be loaded and shipped to a final resting place or salvage yard. They were a wonder then and again now. I was on a random island, isolated and solitary, at a nonspecific time and day, miles and weeks to the south, watching the gates meander past me, far from where they operated for a century.

How did things and time so align that I saw these lock gates twice, in two separate distant places on the same river, as they ended their work life? The four immense structures operated in harmony for ten decades. They had little recognition but were vitally important while doing their job perfectly over their life span.

The lock gates sat in Mississippi River water for a hundred years, opening, closing, then repeating many times a day, frozen in ice all winter, smothered in water. I saw them, at the locks working, as I paddled through. As I observed vessels locking at night, I saw them on the visitor's land deck. I saw them again, at the locks, waiting by a hoist. Then I saw them a last time, miles southbound, days and weeks later, when they were out of water, riding on the river like humans.

Maybe they enjoyed their cruise on the southbound barge like people on Sunday morning pontoons. But I will never know what it was like, where they were going, or where they are now. The life of gates and humans, not knowing everything we wish we knew. We can only guess.

CHAPTER 14

Watershed and War

The convergence of the Bad Axe with the Mississippi River is violent and loud during flooding. But when I paddled on that stretch of pool nine, south of lock & dam eight toward the confluence, I saw a sand bar with a gentle rise. It was considerable enough to land smoothly on top and eat some trail lunch. As I rested there, I thought about the Bad Axe and my long relationship with its movements and branches that ran quietly below my family farm, where I raised sheep for many years. I was grateful to experience its end stream near my sand bar that day and where it made gentle noises while sliding into the downbound Mississippi River.

In an ultimate gravitational feat, our farm ponds and pastures were part of the massive Mississippi River Watershed. They drained gently through a shape of ground that resembled a comma and then downward into the branch before eventually becoming part of the Mississippi. The big river continued to take on water from the Wisconsin, Missouri, and Ohio Rivers and other tributaries of lesser capacity.

My property's water, rain flow through the barns, and flooded road water collectively ran down paths in the fields to the ponds. It then washed through the woods in the comma shape to the main stems, the Mississippi to the Gulf of Mexico, and the oceans and seas of the world where it evaporated and returned to its beginning. It would come down as raindrops, all without assistance from machines or human ingenuity.

The water loop gives life to humans, animals, and plants without prejudice, something meaningful to me because I saw it and knew it most days when I lived on the ridgetop. Humans do not give life to the water cycle, but the reverse is true. Turning on the faucet in our farmhouse kitchen drew water from the well, over three-hundred-fifty feet down, where surface water seeped through four sandstone layers. It filtered impurities before settling as groundwater in darkened spaces below. One thing we trusted every day, the water was clear and pure, always cold, icy cold, right out of the spigot.

If underground water reservoirs, also called aquifers, become emptied, the water has not been used up or lost but moved by human use or misuse. It is somewhere else on Earth - too much in one place, not enough in another. Misappropriation of water frightens and threatens people with flood or drought, death, and disaster. This is how it goes when humans break a law of nature's balance without knowing how to put it back together, like Humpty Dumpty and his unknowing men.

Not a human invention, the watershed phenomenon is a marvel without our help and attention or meddling. It just keeps doing this alone. The only support it accepts is from gravity, ground filtering, momentum, and pressure. It asks for no help from people as it provides everything we need - food, purification, transportation, sanitation, cooling, hydration, swimming, lubricating, quenching, irrigating, and cooking. Another of its gifts was the unforgettable downstream movement of my kayak.

On the farm, water management was a day and night job. At the rise of a high hill, momentum and gravity worked around the clock to take the watershed down to the river. Its moisture brought livestock to drink on mushy pasture, caused hoof rot and made alfalfa moldy. Worms and other parasites crowded into wet places, looking to do harm. The watershed is a reason for battle on dry farmland, but the saving grace of damp land, and it is everything to the river confluence.

After having an apple, almonds, and warm juice, I pushed away from the Bad Axe sand bar. I was eager to move beyond the next bend but hesitated at the two river convergence beside me, near the sand where I had just rested. It was the quiet trickle and peace I found, the junction I was waiting for, usually consistently fast, full of sound and consequence where it goes, but this one was soothing, contemplative, and unpretentious.

Despite my momentary peace, I knew from my study that war occurred in early August at this river mile a hundred and ninety years ago. This was the Bad Axe Massacre when the United States Army killed many Fox and Sauk, five hundred total numbered at the closure of the Black Hawk War. The fighting occurred in the river and adjoining shores when the

United States and its native allies engaged in a land dispute with Indigenous tribes.

The army troops were nearly triple in numbers, but only five U.S. Army soldiers were killed. Casualties were more immense among the native fighters. The win against the native people has been called ferocious and devastating over the decades. So much contradicts what I witnessed during my calm, peaceful respite on the jut out that day.

Paddling along the river below the mouth of the Bad Axe, I was especially struck by its haunted beauty. The battle at Bad Axe occurred right there, and now other temporal attributes around the river are named for it. Blackhawk County Park, Town of Victory, Battle Bluff, Battle Hollow, Battle Island, and Blackhawk Campground are only some.

I knew the paradox as I had rested on the sand, enjoying lunch. I was at the confluence, the joining of two rivers, waters from many places, including my land where sheep had quietly grazed. This place combines water and land between Minnesota on the west and Wisconsin to the east. I felt the combat and horror that still hovers there over the water. I knew the DNA of those who suffered was still in the soil, the river's bed, and maybe the air I breathed.

A steamboat sat right where I was paddling, but those hundred and ninety years before. It attacked the retreating Sauk and Fox as some fled toward Minnesota for safety while others were forced to remain on the Wisconsin side. Women with children were stopped and assaulted in the water. Chiefs Black Hawk and White Cloud encouraged their people to move north for refuge amidst the Ho-Chunk. But the frenzy pushed them to scramble across the river, for whatever reason, maybe confused perseverance, fear, or disorientation from the battle when the night was dark as war. The slaughter lasted hours, two days in total.

The steamboat *Warrior* even left the battle to return to Prairie du Chien for firewood fuel. It took five hours to return upriver and commence fighting. Indigenous people trying to escape the slaughter through the river were killed or drowned right there where I sat in my boat that sunny day.

This was a ruthless and fierce fight to hold on to land that sat quietly in front of my kayak, with hardly anyone aware of what happened there. The history of heartlessness against Indigenous people, the cost of the fighting, and the price paid in lives wasted in exchange for land are palpable at the mouth of the Bad Axe River as it joins the scarred Mississippi.

This is an unsettling and disturbing synthesis of complicated things. The peoples of difference, white and Indigenous, the powerful overtaking the powerless, young and old, adults and children, past and present. The natural landscapes, my farm and its pasture filled with rain, the land and water synchronized. Bleeding and drowning for land now campgrounds and highways, uninhabited islands contaminated with the spirit of killing. Unoccupied forests undeserving of hatred, and the juxtaposition of sheep pasture and war on the watershed. There is an after-quiet of death, dread, and shame over this place, but to only those who know. It is surreal to know and surreal to not know.

The word *confluence* and its action mean to come together, joining two or more as one. The trauma of power and racism has been on Earth from the beginning and is pulsating there on the river. Its cycle will continue like the water cycle, on its own forever, unless we interrupt it.

I want to return to the Bad Axe mouth as it flows into the Mississippi River. Many moments of silence are owed to those gone, who fought for life but were killed, drowned, or starved. Children, grandparents, teens, women, men, and babies were brutalized while humans took humans at the river. It is impossible to paddle through this river sweep without remaining silent, speechless, for those memories still there.

CHAPTER 15

My Book

It was a stubborn spring before I launched on my river trip. In early April, motorcycles fresh from winter storage rumbled through the neighborhood, a sure sign of season change. Runners, bikers, strollers, and walkers were all out. It seemed everyone was outdoors trying to blow winter off their backs. It was nearly ninety degrees late that day. Still, a blizzard was heading eastward toward the Mississippi River Valley to bury us under twelve inches of snow.

We had eight inches in La Crosse by the time it was over, but twelve inches fell forty miles to the southeast. It took a day and all night to drop the heavy snow blown into drifts by the twenty-five mph gusts that followed. Despite the whistling winds and whiteout, it was our true custom during a late spring snowstorm to pretend it did not happen.

Very few showed typical winter vigilance for shoveling sidewalks or moving cars to the right side of the street, and no one put their motorcycles back in storage. The city plows did not even back out of their steel barns, leaving roads full of snow heaps and tire ridges. During a visit to my favored kayak launch in the Mississippi sloughs south of town, I saw anglers in fishing boats stubbornly bundled up while it stormed. They sped rapidly through the backwaters, searching for the best fish hole as if it were July, but I could barely see them through the blowing and falling snow.

During the blizzard, I went on a lengthy walk. Bundled for winter but carrying an umbrella, I was prepared for anything. A college student jogged near me at a red light wearing a tiny sports top and spandex, but I turned away, embarrassed of my wintry look. The rainy snow dripped on her phone as she set some music, but smiling privately when the light went green, she dashed off. As I said, if we pretend it's not winter in our region, then it's not.

*   *   *

In a blog for the *Paddling for Hope* website, I wrote about my river trip last fall and this winter season and what it evoked in me. No matter how low the wintery temperature, how long the night wind wheezed, or how much de-icer I cast over the sidewalk, my writing has kept me on the river. Through memory, I paddle under a hot sun, sleep through quiet nights on feral ground, and face uncountable challenges with fond benefits of living outdoors, on the river, as it endlessly goes downstream. But now, as real-time water moves, it is a foot below the thick river ice.

My writing is vicarious, like a surrogate who lived the river more deeply than I, even though it was me who did it. Combining stories of my other travels, from much earlier to now, takes me out of this room where I write in my house. I cannot hear the wind's whistle or even care about the winter freeze because I have been listening to old sounds from times before. The stories emerge from my mind, nearly seventy years of life passing through on its own.

Last summer, in the middle of my kayak trip and after a rest in La Crosse, I left my home region. I paddled forty river miles south and west to Lansing, Iowa. It was a perfect day with no texture to the water. Its surface was flat as iron, so specks of dust and mite-sized debris settled on it like a dirty room. The sprinklings were left undisturbed over its top as if jimmies on a fancy cake. I liked that the only terrain made was from the bow of my kayak as it split through in utter silence, spreading the water into two sharp and defined lines all that day's journey. People call these "eddy lines" if it matters, but there's more to it than that. I was mesmerized as I watched them all day as a complement to my swaying strokes.

I learned that a paddler must wear the kayak, like a body-suit, while keeping their centerline fitted to the path of gravity - forehead to glabella, nose, then lip, chin, and sternum to the belly button. If held plumb, this line prevented capsizing even if wearing my kayak caused a rhythmical wobbling as it sliced downstream. I did it for six hours that day. My only stops, one to lock through at Genoa Lock and Dam and the other while hesitating at the Lansing Bridge before my friend, Shy, shuttled me to camp.

As I drew closer, miles below the locks, the Lansing Bridge stole my focus for reasons of history. It is an old girder bridge with an unsolid surface that hums from rubber friction. Un-like an asphalt top, the water far below is seen through it. I remember the bridge and its sounds when my family drove over it when I was a girl. We were going the sixty-eight miles to K-mart for school shoes after the store opened in 1964, the year the Beatles came to America.

The bridge has persisted against time since 1931. It only closed for twelve years in the mid-century for ice damage too costly to repair and, for a moment, in 2011 for an unsafe crack. It has seen decades of high and turbulent water, with hundreds, if not thousands, of barges, fishing boats, and recreational craft floating beneath. But now, the old bridge holds a secret. Its life will end in 2024 when the replacement bridge is built, seven years short of its hundredth birthday. I, for one, will cry a tear for the Black Hawk Bridge and thank Shy for taking our picture in its center as we crossed, with traffic bearing down both ways.

No one can argue that its design is plain. From afar, it appears it was made with an Erector Set. The narrowness is startling as it arches up and back when driven over. Even though the girders are heavy steel beams, from my kayak below, they appeared thin, like delicate wire. But a rare straight-on look from its broadside was a pure marvel, so unique and inspiring as I wondered how it was ever constructed. The fine-designed outline is incredible, so light that it's remarkable it has kept itself up. I paused my kayak in the water to view the breathtaking angle and became acutely aware I would not be in this position or moment again any time soon. The bridge is rich in simpleness and complexity, of both age and reliability.

The Lansing Bridge grabbed the heart of another back home, so much so that they chose it as a champion landmark to uphold the message of *Paddling for Hope* - equity, unity, and fair balance - that we seek in our upriver community and the far-reaching world. I feel grateful to the donor whose heart moved to love the bridge, give in its name, and contribute to the message that my river trip embodied.

After paddling many miles with little rest that day, I felt fatigued. I finally left the water at Big Slough Landing, where Shy picked me up for camp. We stopped for supper food and set up my gear. Then Shy left me at my tent site, where I spent two nights and two days in seclusion. I listened to water ripples at the bottom of a ravine behind me and read the only book I brought in my kayak about a boundless person as a spirit.

I wandered the small roads around my camp and heard sounds produced by everything but humans. My only companions were the trickling water below, a dog across the ravine that barked in the night, and my book. It was perfect enough. That is how those many hours alone went before Shy returned me to the river.

By the first morning, in my camp chair with coffee and the book, I had wet hair from an early shower, nowhere to be, and nothing to do except read. Anyone would covet my situation for at least a moment, but I had another fifteen hours before sleep would come. Time was insipidly still, with no wind, clouds, or rain. It was simple and complete, but only sometimes felt like it. I was distracted by bird tweets, distant cars on the road, and looping thoughts. Once, a small plane flew over.

Solitude is a spiritual and cerebral undertaking often ruined by busyness and electronics that make us busier now than before. I forgot my charging equipment in Shy's car, so my phone was out of power. I wondered what I would gain from this isolation with no communication with the outside world and no preoccupation with the internet. I turned my attention to the never-silent creek below that offered good background harmony at no cost and this only book I brought in my kayak.

When I opened it, I saw inside the cover the date I first began reading it, in 2013, but I left it forgotten on a shelf for the next nine years. I did not neglect it because of a lack of interest, a dull subject matter, or a language other than my own. I might have left the book untouched because I was busy or preoccupied with the needs and antics of humans. But now, I could read through my river trip with complete concentration to capture its soulful essence. The time was given to me today, yesterday, two nights, and again tomorrow for reading this old book, copyrighted in 1910, and my edition was nearly fifty years old.

The dark red cover was intact but with worn nubs at its corners and on the spine where it was fingered by someone before me. The pages were dry and easily cracked, and the author died almost a century ago. My only option was this book, which smelled old and brittle. Nothing else was here. It was the only book with no people, electricity, or lights for the night. I did not need to cook food or buy it already made, and no one was here to speak with or watch from across the road. I heard this in my mind - *it is for you, your time, your boundless person*. But *for what exactly*, I wondered.

Is it better to be alone, like in a jail cell, lost in a cave, or isolated in a tiny space capsule? In the end, there was no room for discussion or negotiation. Only me, my book, and the creek noise with the dog bark and a random bird. I already took my third shower, so I turned to my book. I opened it again, a genuine and actual book with a woven spine under glued paper, once read years ago. Then I glanced up in case a person arrived. No humans, so I returned to the book.

*   *   *

I remembered a campground up far north where I stayed for two nights. There were showers there, too, and I needed the relaxation of a second day, called a "zero-day" by paddlers. I arrived on a weekday, so only three campers were parked across the sizeable grassy property. Its shape was of a beaker whose wide bottom sat to the south, and the top spout sat to the north, where my camp was set snug. My tent was on the rise of the high riverbank and cornered on two sides by the Mississippi River, snaking from east going west, then eventually north again.

Over those two days, I sat with my book open but watched the campground fill with all types of machinery. Because my site was on the narrow top of the beaker, I could sit quietly and watch people pull in, set up, and begin their play and leisure. At the same time, I listened to the Mississippi River, relatively narrow at this point, as it rippled by and turned its corner as I tried to read my book. The large boat ramp was one campsite away, where I launched after two days. Besides easy access to the shower and getting good rest, I learned something else while sitting there. People like their stuff and take it wherever they go. The Iowa campground reinforced it, where I thought I was stranded but really was not.

I had a tent and kayak on my site at the northern campground, the only tent in nine available campsites by my first day there. The local campers occupied seven spaces, each with a large RV and other motorized objects. It was a parking lot of RVs, pull-behind vehicles, motorcycles, and watercraft tugged on the back. One family pulled a storage trailer that opened, and piles of belongings spilled out when the door released to the ground – a sandbox, badminton, roller blades, bicycles, and a tree swing. I remembered just a few.

People removed oversized barbeque grills from RV storage and set them beside their RV doors. This way, cooking was just like at home. There were many distractions, and dogs that owners incessantly called loudly *get back here!* I observed their efforts and became preoccupied, too, but I tried to return to my book.

When I left that northern camp and paddled west on the river, it was calm – both the river and my mind. I felt the same when Shy picked me up in Iowa to take me back to the river. My next launch was near a casino and under a large bridge. Both times, way north and in Iowa, it was exhilarating to return to the river, rested and full of thought about humans and my book explaining life spirit.

Humans are life, good and true, filled with knowledge that is not our own, not mine, or belonging to any human. It is of nature and energy that moves without me, not with a motor or fuel or any idea that comes from uncomplicated reasoning. It is of truth and wisdom, not organic life or understanding, which is always beyond what people naturally think. The book said it is about promises.

There are giant stars, young and old, more compressed than anything ever seen or touched by living beings, and the largest belongs to a supercluster that is beyond anything a human can comprehend. It is a promise of the most significant magnitude. We only think that this could be true. It is energy where new stars are formed regularly, not news or a surprise, but the most enormous promise, chief of all. It is more significant than any Milky Way galaxy, universe, heavens, or all the giant stars together.

Our biggest unsolvable concerns and problems, and our needs and thoughts that take up so much room, unable to give while taking, we are constantly searching. I neglected the book for years because it was difficult to grasp at a glance. It is beyond philosophy, psychology, science, logic, or the natural world. It is overwhelming and cannot be read with distractions or other noise in the room.

*   *   *

Back in the north, the river was calm below my camp because the nearby town became weary after a great flood and built a diversion channel to reroute flood water. The riverbed makes large serpentine twists, and the community sits at the bottom of one curling U-shaped portion. It was a cinch for gravity to pour flood waters into the bottom of the U, where people were most populated, as easy as dumping water from a bucket.

To win over gravity, engineers dug a ruler-straight six-mile channel across the top of the U to divert flooding Mississippi River waters. It was re-introduced to the river in smaller cup portions at various downstream locations. I paddled the river above the diversion channel and again below. So I witnessed a marked difference in speed, amplitude, and the pleasant flow and mood of the water's surface that first morning I left. The diversion channel took the fury out of the river like a lobotomy. It was a mighty feat for humans to achieve control of water and its volume, scope, and damage to towns filled with people. I saw where small amounts were dribbled back into the downbound direction of the river over a long distance.

As I kayaked quietly on the water that day, my thoughts and concerns about homogenous river populations did not leave me. They came up naturally and occasionally, then stayed at length other times. People groups have historically clashed and continually struggled with each other. Despite their serene appearances, the communities along the Mississippi River were no different. One location, in particular, was where Enbridge's Line 3 pipeline crossed under the river, carrying tar sands oil to U.S. refineries. I am aware that everyone uses fuel and other energy resources. Most people would holler if it was gone or not easily accessible at home or in their vehicles. But no human has a perfect method of unearthing, moving, or utilizing it, especially if honoring the "do no harm" principle.

Even so, the pipeline construction risked immediate environmental menaces. Wetlands and other bodies of water were in danger in the case of a spill. A significant oil spill from another Enbridge pipeline in Michigan filled the Kalamazoo River with over a million gallons of the same crude oil. Whether in Northern Minnesota, Michigan, or anywhere, the pipeline crosses habitats for native and migratory birds and other diverse species.

The installation threatened the ancestral lands and wild rice beds of Indigenous people. Treaty violations multiply around this Line 3 pipeline, so the insult goes deep into the heart and back into history, whether we admit it or not. The need for access roads, machinery, and stringing pipes caused the clearing of untold acres of forested land that belong to Indigenous people and their communities, the disruption of crane nesting and rookeries, and trauma to vast wildlife living there. The future had been challenged.

As I traveled through, I saw large and bright-colored protest signs, even after the pipeline was completed and pumping hundreds of thousands of barrels daily under this quiet, natural, and sacred land. The infraction seems unforgivable because no one has apologized or agreed that a violation against humans and nature occurred. So, hearts remain heavy, and few are paying attention anymore.

A few days later, it was beautiful and peaceful when I paddled on the Mississippi River toward Crow Wing. I kayaked forty-five miles that day and met up with only two people, a couple in a fishing boat who spoke to me with interest. Otherwise, it was a wild and isolated place. There were occasional well-maintained summer homes on the shoreline but no people.

Eventually, the nature of dwellings transformed into small villages of aged RVs and rusty campers, old buses, and shacks used for permanent housing. Some were caving under the constant moisture of river humidity. I passed several of these villages, and the only signs of life were a man exiting a pit toilet and four Indigenous children laughing and playing on a muddy and tilted trampoline.

The difference between the well-maintained and spacious houses and these collapsing overcrowded communities was harsh on these same miles of river. I was paddling for hope, for a change of hearts in all people to embrace that everyone is worthy, whether well-resourced or not. I was kayaking through another great divide with my book about boundlessness and abundance. My heart was getting heavier.

I paddled all day thinking about people and earmarked Lone Pine as my next camp. After traveling twenty-two miles downriver from last night's camp, I spotted the campsite from the opposite riverbank and paddled crosscurrent to it. The wood-braced steps into Lone Pine were soupy mud from flooding, but I tried them anyway. I slipped and skidded to the camping area and found the air gray and dense with mosquitos. The ground was weak and muddy, also soaked by flood water, so I had to move on. The next camp, Half Moon, was eighteen river miles further, and it was nearing dusk already. So I started paddling again, hoping for better at Half Moon. But when I reached it, the ground was underwater.

I messaged Vicki, whose river home was only four more miles downstream. She had invited me for the next night, but I made it sooner after passing these two soggy camps. Vicki's response was enthusiastic and welcoming, so I quickened my strokes and arrived about a half hour later.

* * *

This family waiting downriver was my first River Angel host. Their original invitation came before I left home and after they had heard I would be traveling downriver. *Our home is open,* Vicki said, if I wanted to stop. Of course, a shower after sliding on mud-filled steps and paddling for hours, a bed, a meal, and laundry were all appealing by then. Although it was awkward to walk into someone's home as a stranger with a laundry bag on my shoulder and sit down for supper. The River Angel standard does not expect or accept any payment for their hospitality, so I wasn't entirely sure why they were open to inviting strangers. But I learned quickly.

While in their home, I was welcomed openly and unreluctantly. I was there less than twenty-four hours, but the family shared so considerably that all agreed we must have known one another in a different lifetime. I read in the book of Hebrews *to help people by welcoming them into your home, being friendly, pleasant, and gracious, sharing your comforts, and doing your part bigheartedly.* This family naturally knew how this should go and lived it out liberally, as other River Angels did up and down the Mississippi River.

Two home-cooked meals, a good night's rest, clean laundry, and good conversation restored and energized me. When they sent me off downriver, I was grateful for River Angels, these and all the others, ever-present, reaching out and welcoming with offers of assistance.

Vicki reminded me that the next dam was a hard right turn and beyond a bridge. It seemed incidental then, but nothing was insignificant once I arrived there. I paddled fifteen miles over wide bodies of water, sharing Sunday morning with anglers and pleasure boaters toward the approach to Brainerd.

*   *   *

I saw something in the distance and came upon a small, flat-bottomed boat. Inside were three men, moving about, changing places, and anchored near the side of a large cove. From afar, it was impossible to know their details, so I mistakenly counted four people in the boat, but one was the sizeable outboard motor. When I was close to it, the inhabitants became obvious. Three gray-haired men fishing.

They stopped all commotion to stare as I slowly paddled

near them. Their heads turned deliberately in unison as they watched me, my head rotating toward them. I was given complete attention by all three the same. They seemed to be wondering about me as I also thought about them. Then I realized it. These three men were brothers, identical, even dressed alike, with matching hats. They were triplet brothers, about eighty-five years old, staring like silent boys with matching thin smiles.

I nodded, said nothing, and kept going. The three men were as amazed that I was just me as I was astonished that they were equally alike. None of us spoke, yet we found each other memorable that morning. A short distance beyond, I turned to look back at them. They were still motionless, staring as I went, their interest following me downriver.

I came upon a bridge shortly after the triplet brothers and saw a structure up ahead, afterward of the bridge, but it did not register that I had reached the Potlatch Dam. I used my rangefinder to prove it, and there it was, confirmed. I could see the aroused mist in the air, rising high and beyond the dam as flood waters poured aggressively through the rollers in the downstream direction. I hugged the right bank and slowly eased closer, hoping to avoid the pull of the downbound current that could suck me into the dam.

As I inched, the booming sound of dam-released water, smoky high-rising vapor, and swiftly moving suds was disturbing. I sat straight up to be vigilant for any possibility before me while creeping closer to the dam structure. I could not see a way out or a portage take-out expected on the right bank. A tree-covered point protruded just enough to create a blind spot before impact with the dam wall thirty meters to the front. I hoped the take-out was somewhere between.

At the last moment, a large sign emerged from the brush announcing the portage ahead by a twisted chain-link fence and wooden tie-up. It seemed plenty to brace against if necessary. I abruptly turned and pushed up on land, secured my boat, and then took position up the slope to assess its layout. What I needed to do was clear, but I walked through it for good measure before emptying my boat and hauling my gear uphill. At the far end of the portage, I found the only put-in site next to the release of surging waters from Potlatch Dam. The side waters were boiling chaotically, like lava, with white caps and suds on top. A sign cautioning against careless portaging warned about Class 3 rapids during post-flooding.

I called for local marine assistance, seeking a second opinion or to be moved to a safer launch. The dispatcher said it could be hours before someone arrived due to multiple flooding complaints. When I returned to the take-out, I saw another boat had just pulled in and was tying off. It was a father-son canoe team I had met upriver, where we had spontaneously set up camp near each other. In hindsight, realizing they were very close behind me through our day's journey was a comfort.

The presence of companions did not change the waters, but it gave a second opinion and mutual assistance if something went wrong. After assessments at the dam portage, we put our boats on the churning shoreline together and shoved off against the boiling rapids. It was a great ride, fast but safe, as we were carried downstream. My fellow paddlers planned to make camp just above Crow Wing, where I was welcomed to join them for the night, an invitation I gratefully accepted. The remainder of the day was pleasant as we paddled the fifteen miles parallel but separate and eager to set up camp.

*   *   *

It could have been the wind, the hot sun, or the salty trail mix and jerky I packed. Add the pressure of the Potlatch Dam waters, and I had an unquenchable thirst for an ice-cold carbonated drink, which took a prominent place in my thoughts throughout the all-day paddle. I saw a mini-mart on the map and off-river, but it was only a short walk if I could find a place to tie up. I paddled the miles toward the location and thought constantly about a cold pop filled with ice. I was not kidding. I was on a quest. My thirst for something icy cold had become severe. I added a lunchtime meal, dessert, and something extra, like a handful of candy bars, to my forthcoming food stop if I could find a take-out point to go ashore and then walk to the store.

My friends paddled with me as we leapfrogged one another all afternoon. They passed me on one occasion and asked how I was doing. I yelled over. *I'm praying for a cold pop!* I was unsure how that was received, but I meant what I said. Yet it was improbable that a cold beverage would materialize out of nowhere on this long stretch of warm and remote river.

I did not find a boat ramp near the alleged store, which forced me to suppress my desire for the icy carbonated drink. We ended the day on the right bank over Crow Wing territory. Despite one of my companion's uneasiness with resident snakes, we set up a comfortable night camp. I had given up on a cold drink and was in my sleeping bag by late evening.

Later, I heard my friend outside my tent asking, *do you*

want this? I unzipped the flap and saw an ice-cold bottle of Coke in his hand. I was unsure if it was a mirage, an obsessive dream, or the promise in my red book, the energy of provision beyond human grasp. It tasted perfect and was an assured supply wherever it came from. I learned the landowner had come with snacks, including the icy Coke. I slept well that night, my thirst quenched, and the mysterious promise was kept.

*   *   *

These were times about people before the Black Hawk Bridge and the many miles I traveled to get there. I sat in my chair with the red book still open, with hours of reading behind me. I looked back over the river and my time spent alone but with people included in extraordinary ways. I saw human lives along the river – the camps lavished with gear, mud villages, poverty and riches, disturbed sacred ground, grand homes, companionship, night camps, generous angels, three old triplets, and an ice-cold drink out of nowhere. These were the events of those days, nothing treacherous when it could have been, everything surprisingly welcoming and full, more than asked for and much more than expected.

I was not secluded on the river when alone or with people. There was energy and the time of movement and truth that never ceased. I made none of it happen or change, with no power or intention. The searching and finding, pure like fire, consuming and illuminating, warming and cooling, all is beyond me, but for me. Not alone but by myself and blessed with others. And I had my book.

CHAPTER 16

Trees on the River

As I paddled my kayak down the river and through the merging pool of these two greats, the Wisconsin and Mississippi, it evoked memories and emotions from a visit I had experienced to this place before. It was years ago, but on land then, not by water, and with my young dog Ruthie. These potent recollections of the past deepened as I drew slowly along this stretch of water on the Iowa side while on my river trip. My preoccupation prevailed for hours while paddling as I drifted and gazed up toward the ridges to the east. Ruthie and I had camped on that highest ridge for many days in the late season, just before winter, many years ago.

*   *   *

I was a younger adult when I left my city home for a long trip away to camp at the backside and distant point above the river valley. It was close to my birth home, with over fifty years of history and family visits there. Besides the Mississippi, I always favored the Upper Iowa River nearby, the Turkey and

Yellow Rivers, plus the Volga when I had the time. The dog and I had camped several nights at various places and explored by day. But for a few of those nights, we stayed high on this ridge I was just passing beneath while paddling the river during my 2022 river trip. I placed my previous camp on a flat rise near the forested perimeter of a vacated group camp and at the highest place on the ridge. During my recent paddle journey, I hoped to avoid the chaos of that previous camp when choosing a riverside spot with my kayak in tow.

During our land trip and first overnight, a populated raccoon family called a Gaze kept me awake until near dawn. I listened to their scavenging through garbage cans and firepits, finding anything left by late autumn campers. This went on for several hours in the dark. The critters made a real ruckus, like a hoard of children upstairs who refused to go to bed.

When I peered out the zipper flap with my camp light, I saw a large raccoon tripping over a sack of cookies caught between their legs while escaping toward the woods. They dragged it by mouth, dropping pieces as they stumbled. Others were snarling and following fast, wanting some cookies, too. I listened carefully in case these feisty animals moved my way, but I was likewise glad for the company in a dark and quiet place. I had not gotten used to it yet, and Ruthie was a bit edgy too.

It was nearing sunrise when the raccoon feast ended, and I heard little slapping strikes on my tent, but then we fell into a sound and pleasant sleep. The sun was just up when I woke to a thick layer of wet, icy snow and raccoon mess. The snow was filled with ice beads tiny as flyspecks that hit tersely on my tent fly while it was still dark. It sounded like flicking fingers on a taut kite skin but was dull enough to sleep through.

The ice bits caused snow to melt quickly, creating a squishiness underfoot as we walked the trails later, soaking Ruthie's paws to about ankle-high. It pushed her into the scrubby edge along the path to walk more easily. Despite this, it was so good and sweet to be in the midst of a wild place like that.

*　　*　　*

During my recent paddle journey, I scouted a favorable camp below this ridge where Ruthie and I had previously slept, but this time, I was alone and coming in by water. While exploring for a base camp, I saw a tree with a hole in its bark face. The tree was old with girth and rose up from a ravine below me. The hole opening was sizeable and about thirty feet from the root flare. The impressive bulge of the trail caught me at eye-level with the tree hole where a great horned owl stared at me, many meters into the wooded ravine. It glared at me without a blink, so I lowered the bow of my kayak mid-portage to watch back. The focus between us was mesmerizing, so intense that it appeared the owl was also thinking about how it was.

I slowly lifted my boat and began lightly walking but continued to scrutinize the owl's colossal face. It had no neck, but its eyes were as round as plates, golden like honey, and a body at least two feet tall that did not overfill the massive tree hole. The owl's gaze remained locked on me as I continued down the trail and eventually got to my work toward a night camp.

Hours later, after I had set up my things, I returned a different way and walked along a valley of rocks. I rimmed the river sloughs filled with deadwood and tree roots where many water birds were fishing – herons, egrets, and a green night heron above me in the ragged overhang of a riverbank tree. The stagnant water was dark green-brown and decaying, producing a raw smell. It was awesomely quiet against my footsteps while I had that owl on my mind. I felt affection for it living there, fending alone and doing what it was made to do.

The final stretch of path was uphill, over the same ground I wheeled my boat when looking for night camp. As I passed over the trail incline across from the old tree, I looked toward the hole. There it was, the same owl staring at me like it had never moved and was expecting me. I didn't stare back this time but felt reverence for its tranquility and tolerance to stay, the opposite of human multi-tasking and constant movement. I envied the owl and have thought of it many times since. I had a remarkable encounter with that great horned owl and ancient tree.

Back at camp, I prepared for the night and fell asleep early. At dawn, I heated water for coffee outside my tent while watching four piliated woodpeckers spread wide across a growth of mature oaks and maple behind me. I sat on my sleep gear with a hot cup to see them flit, then tap and dig for morning food, different from the motionless owl, but more like humans doing morning busyness. Besides their rapping sounds and agitated outcries that lacked a melody, my time there was quiet.

The thick tree stand of white and black oaks and old maples was surrounded by more delicate maple saplings and new black walnuts. They covered sloping ground in a crescent shape around and away from my camp. My mind was on the trees and how they supply shelter, food, and protection for many animals. Each part of every tree gives something all the time. They never stop.

*　　*　　*

While working my way downriver in my kayak, I replayed mental recollections from the years before. I thought about humans plodding quietly across the ridges above me, thousands of people over as many years. Some went right through the trees I camped beneath before I returned to my boat and where Ruthie and I had slept during our early year when it snowed. Both times, an elusive trace in the air was barely noticeable. Even though it was solid and potent, I'm unsure whether Ruthie detected it the same as I did. It was a visceral residue of something that had remained for centuries.

When paddling the confluence during my river trip, I was hugging the riverbank because of the dangerous rough water made rougher by weekend boaters, and I was thinking about trees. I loved traveling and sleeping under great river trees like Hackberry and Silver Maple with some Cottonwood still releasing its seed. At the face of one near-vertical ridge, the trees were wild, dense, and unmanaged like a child's morning hair. This was amazing, mainly as it reflected the bright morning sun strikes.

As I rounded a bend in the Mississippi River that was full and energized as it blended with the Wisconsin River, it continued south and smoothed eastward to a side slough protected from the rough water and wind. The sudden stillness caused me to feel unsettled inside, as quivering jelly, after the constant thudding of irregular waves and motored boats that I was accustomed to on the river's main channel. So I took a short rest.

I knew pure stands of Black Walnut were around me, but when things were fully green, they were nearly impossible to detect. But the black crooked walnut limbs were dramatic and noticeable when they were bare during my early winter visit. I finally felt blessed and calm when I realized I was in hidden beauty, where I hoped to catch a gust of walnut odor. Much like at Marching Bear mounds when with Ruthie years before, the tall trunks rose from below, passed by me, and went high into a canopy this time of year. At first and quick glance, they seemed even daintier than before and too slim for their height. Oddly thick and thin, the forestry was sufficient for my camp's heavy populace of pileated woodpeckers.

Below the tall trees at the river edge, I noticed the well-worn Wisconsin and Mississippi River Valley footpaths were hardened by human feet, yet the place remained quiet as ever. No people. A mood infused the air during my stay there. Neither good nor bad, just heavy and unmistakable, with a strong feeling I was not alone anywhere I set out.

Maybe it was the hope that early people left behind or their worry and expectations as they crossed the same geography as we do now. They pulled supplies or their wounded, maybe bundled babies, on travois of handcrafted branch wood and bark. Later, others used wagons with wheels or, like now, all-terrain vehicles that run loud with motors. We all have left parts of ourselves behind, like food scraps, bag cookies, plastics, fumes and litter, energy, lost stamina, or some of our cells.

*   *   *

When I was there with my dog, Ruthie, we crossed the bridge to hike up the Iowa-side ridge facing east of the river.

We used the Marching Bear trail to reach the burial mounds, an ascent of nearly five-hundred-seventy-five feet. I remember that the path switched back enough to avoid extra steep portions, and besides, Ruthie needed the run. The ridges skirting our walk splayed downward steeply on all sides and away from the almost-petrified dirt trail. They were thick with leftover summer overgrowth and tall, handsome trees vibrant with sugary color still clinging. It was humid only because of that waterlogged snow that had filled the air and footpaths with loose moisture that morning.

My dog and I were worn when the trail leveled at a small meadow near the top. Ruthie was small, barely past a retriever pup, tempting a red-tail hawk to circle above, wanting her for something. The hawk spotted Ruthie because hawks do that when they see a little animal running around like a playful rabbit. This meant lunch to a large hungry bird, so I hurried Ruthie into the trees toward the first mound. We rested then, sitting along the treeline and eating lunch with some cool water. There, the trees were our shelter, some shade, and protection.

I stared at the first grand burial mound, an outstretched eagle, near our lunch spot. It could have been at least three feet high and a hundred feet long. At its opening, I realized a large pile of long red hair heaped in the grass and definitely human. I looked intently at it, distracted from the mound, and wondered whose it was and why it was there. Again, a supernatural current suddenly whipped up through the wet air, electricity maybe, as I looked far out over the river, the near confluence, and Wisconsin beyond that.

The essence was solid and stable, surrounding us while

we slept the night before near trees on the other side. While hiking up the bear mounds trail and padding past the human hair pile at the opening, the spirits of bears, the immense raised eagle, and more natural currents were in the wind. This was slight but vital energy, not scary or repelling, but gentle and almost nonexistent. I felt Ruthie and I were caught in its influence. Hanging leaves were almost entirely gone, except for the oaks whose stubborn leathery ones refused to drop. They rattled in the unexpected breeze.

To see the mounds and imagine thousands of years before that moment when I was sitting with lunch and my dog, ancient people meandered about with children and elderly, passing food while working and bounded by their dead. I had entered this. It had not moved into me. It was old and sound, a profound experience of something greater than me as one lone human with a pup, more so than our present-day world going to and fro on the river road below, barge traffic trudging on the water channel, and the dense trees we followed to get up there. It was a felt sense that was not ignored or forgotten. I was not afraid to sleep near this place or feel it as it naturally presented. My interest persisted in the experience of birds, all the creatures in the walnut forest, the thousands of trees, and the leftover snow, with a sense that someone and something was drifting through all the days and nights, but not because I was there. They have been coming and going all along.

As I enjoyed the earlier morning at my wintry campsite, I imagined Indigenous people padding along those forested trails long ago and before now. They seemed to be floating. I felt the human spirit of the movement in the brush as it noiselessly passed. At Spook Hill, the burial mounds are dutifully kept, still from long before, and evidence of the Hopewell Tribe and Red Ocher culture are found in the forests because both were woodland people who built mounds that are still intact today. Trappers and traders followed through much later, jangling pack animals clunking behind along with these workers' hopes to make a living. When Indigenous and European people intersected there, the Black Walnut forest and the early humans of both were bundled with enthusiasm, courage, and heart with immense grit. It was from these early people that the confluence of the Wisconsin and Mississippi Rivers was regarded as a neutral zone where peace and sharing were had, which could be why I felt peace there, even during sleep in a spirit-active realm.

*　　*　　*

All trees, even those where I have been before, give gifts and blessings. I always love them, never taking them for granted or as any nuisance. Trees are everything, maybe more than even wind. They give shade, food, a place for creatures, tea leaves, medicine, firewood, furniture, syrups, fruit, bark, nuts, and peels. They do not ask for much but to be left alone to grow and offer, and they move when the wind says.

I could go on all day with this about trees because their uses and gifts are perpetual. It is obvious that trees give life and are life. They are living energies, giving, spewing out all kinds of spirit that weave through branches, stems, and time, through little limbs and leaves, then down to touch us on the ground. Their roots grab and go under the earth to hang on and sustain themselves. They are tangles, like nets, that hold the shadows of past movements and people, caught to enrich the place they went through. We often need details about the greatness of trees, maybe so much more than what we get about humans.

When paddling my kayak or camping nearby on the water, my experience always combines trees and rivers. I realize it's because my rootedness is to the Upper Mississippi River region where I was born, where I returned, and where so much wooded land is adjacent to the river. Some river locations are bordered by factories, industry, open farmland, desert, or less forested wild land. My love of the north remains profound even when paddling those different regions and even when they reveal their astonishing traits. There really is no place to return to but where we took root. Mine is the Mississippi River Valley and its Driftless Region.

CHAPTER 17

Spiders

While planning my river trip, I worried about random night fears, going out there alone, creepy critters of my make-believe, and the most horrible giant spiders. But the thought of snakes didn't bother me at all. As the trip and planning went on, I had fear-filled moments of imagined things, but some were in noticeably evident form.

No intruders of any significance came near me except a little sniffy-nosed creature at the outside corner of my tent one night. It was where my food was stored inside a bear bag and next to me while I slept. Despite being against camping norms and not very smart, I occasionally kept my food bag for easy access and admit I was lazy those evenings. I didn't feel like troubling myself to hang it or devise a plan to keep my provisions or me secure from animals. But no matter what, tucking food near me is taboo in the outdoor world. Sleeping with it, even in crumb form, invites danger. I was out of bear country, where skulking animals are large and extra hungry as the snow melts, so I trusted my conclusion. After my little visitor in my nighttime riverbank camp, even though innocent enough, I changed my habits with the provision bag.

Its makers say it's made of a material stronger than bears, an ultra-high-molecular-weight polyethylene called UHMWP, and theoretically impervious to bullets and bears. Yet when tested, a bear's sharp tooth caught up in the sturdy weave without a rip or the skill to open the sack, even after food smells lured it there. If suitably twisted around a tree or picnic table's leg, no bear would have luck dragging the bag back to the den unless they took the table, too.

Mice were said to find their way in at the knotted pull cord around the top much better than any more giant mammal. These fast, tiny critters can ruin a mess sack worse than any bear. No gear is perfect, but this bear bag almost is - like my Delta kayak - or at least it was for my purposes on my river trip. As I ate down my food volume, the bag shape-shifted, smaller and smaller, unlike hard-surfaced blue barrels. This feature enabled it to snug further into my hatch.

Despite adding an odor-proof liner, the bear bag quickly drew the snout of this small night animal whose nose looked like a weasel. It sounded like my dog sniffing for crumbs under the kitchen counter or smelling a breeze along the backdoor. Those puffing toots sound like a harmonica, but a dog's snoopiness draws her like that.

As for the wild animal, I never saw its entirety by the end, but I heard it take the tour of other camps, rifling through garbage and left-behind catfish guts by a fire ring. Looking for something better to eat, it made the rounds before heading back to my tent to sniff like a dog again, sneaking a whiff of sweet jerky, so scent-strong it penetrated my protective bag and two walls of the tent.

I swatted at the animal and put lantern light in its face when its nose pushed beneath my rainfly at three in the morning. Whatever the busybody, it was not too hungry since my sleepy and feeble efforts caused it to go. I was proved wrong about food in the tent that could draw an animal so close on my first violation. No other significant thing happened to me with critters except a pile of fresh bear scat close by my tent one night, but it was without the bear.

Mostly, I am very afraid of spiders, so I was initially anxious about how to deal with them on my trip. I posted my spider concerns and questions on the Mississippi River Paddlers' Facebook page, and it confirmed my reasons for worry. I heard paddlers who went the year before me had seen massive spiders in their camps, boats, tents, and clothing. I was mainly unnerved at the thought of one in my tent, inside my sleeping bag with me, or hiding in my boat until I was on the river, unable to slap it as it crawled up my leg. But the sudden surprise of any spider near me anywhere, at a picnic table, on my camp chair, on a footpath shrub, or on my bedroom wall, is a jarring experience for a person like me with spider fear.

On my trip, I saw plenty of spiders out there in the brush and on the water, but only one I fought off in alleged self-defense. Twice, I spotted enormous river spiders walking across the water and toward my boat. Similar to landbound wolf spiders, these hulking spiders can have a five-inch leg span and possess the ability to walk on water surface like a sheet of rippling glass. It is easy to think of them as wicked with a mind full of devious plans, but the animal world is not a made-up fantasy like that.

For the first spider, I measured the distance to shore with my eyes and saw it was a long walk for any spider, so I offered it my paddle as a respite landing. When the spider saw my generous gesture, it behaved like various humans I have known, picking up speed rapidly and running across the water's tension. It aimed precisely at my kayak, possibly thinking only of itself and a more sizable portion than I was offering.

I envisioned it crawling up the hull, into my cockpit, or through my gear, which caused my inner turmoil way out on the river. Unexpectedly, it crossed my mind that *tossing pearls to pigs leads to greed and aggression,* so I grabbed my paddle and slapped at the water, bringing the flat edge down hard. I did not mean to drown the spider, but in urgent haste to stop what I had set in motion, I might have done it.

To the second spider on another day, I did not offer a gesture but kept my distance instead, and that turned out better for both of us. As it crossed the river before me, I swerved my kayak in a half circle around the spider, enabling us each to go our own way. Because it was the season when spiders were preoccupied with hunting and feeding themselves, I tried to keep in mind they were not interested in me.

Wolf and water spiders can scare any living thing, which is the idea. But even without growling, screaming, or bearing large teeth, it is only their size that is disturbing. Several times, I have seen wolf spiders prowling or patiently poised to ambush, and even though not on the river, it is especially unforgettable and creepy.

Most spiders make good neighbors if left alone to make a

nightly web and sleep all day in a hidden corner. By evening, they return to the web to rebuild it, like a human reweaving an old lawn chair. A spider's web is the same, used up then re-spun, each time a little scruffier and more unfocused than before.

We can tell an old spider by the wear of its web. The first night is perfection, but after nights of reconstruction, they forget or are too tired to measure. As time passes and the old, fat spider patches the web, the silk strands lose their refined, delicate design, like worn-out farmer jeans that are over-mended. Looks no longer count, but it gets it done sturdy for one more use.

Like people, spiders get tired as their time draws near and attempts are given less effort. One evening, when the web flutters in a breeze with no revising going on, it is inevitable that the spider is just gone. When I saw this in my river camps, I wondered if they were on to the next thing or just eaten by a bird.

Several times, I saw fattened spiders in my camps at distinct places and on different nights. Big-butted, gray in color, waddling along doing what spiders are supposed to do. As I pitched my tent one evening, I ducked each time I passed under a web while I spread my tent sides to stake them. The web's spider was busy, building steadily with perfection, but I mistook its enthusiastic bouncy motion as clumsiness. The spider was so quick and plump that I thought it might go off balance and fall on my head one of the times I passed under, but I still didn't want to disturb it.

A relief to humans, spiders do not drop under their usual conditions. They are so skilled in hanging on and too focused on themselves and their work to be interested in us. They will make a sticky web, but not for fear of falling because spiders do not stick to their own webbing. The sticky is for us, the invaders, and other food that gets too close.

As a spider-watcher, observation of their ordinary tasks makes any of my fear of them a waste of emotion. The spider rarely thinks of jumping on a human or biting our flesh. Even so, we are afraid a spider on a wall or bush is waiting to jump on us as we go by. But jumping spiders are built differently from non-jumping types, making it easy to discern which it is, so you can duck quickly.

Jumping spiders have many more enormous eyes to aim their leap better and often make silk tethers from themselves to their perch, in case they misjudge. Other variations exist, but these two are the easiest to detect if a person is worried about airborne spiders headed toward them. If not the jumping family of spiders, they will probably not take a jump.

The night of the rotund weaving spider above my tent, I thought we shared this solitude experience. It was alone on the web, and I was alone on the river. Busy each evening putting up our camps, busy each morning taking them down, and me paddling to the new place to do it over again. I will be gone from here one day, just like the spider.

Discovering that a watched-spider has gone is not sad or disappointing, but simply how it is, the fate of nature. It is how life in the world goes. If I had reached the gulf below New Orleans, I imagined it secluded and anticlimactic, like the spider and web. A solitary experience of my own, one that only I would know in that moment and memory. If I had achieved it, I imagine I would have paddled out to the point and turned back with a single turn-around stroke, like a spider knitting the last time and spending a final night in its web.

CHAPTER 18

Wisdom is Diamonds

This is about difficulties on the river that keep paddlers on edge and constantly vigilant. Two things on a river trip are true: life is good, and you never know.

I heard about a paddler admitted to a hospital after heatstroke took its toll. Heat on the river rose over a hundred degrees, and below St. Louis, heat advisories continued with severe life-threatening warnings. Other paddlers reported foot and hand blisters, numbness from paddling, dangerous sunburns, and excessive weight loss when continuous movement could not be balanced with tuna and trail mix.

At about a fourth or a third of the way down this ruthless river, paddlers sometimes feel eager or impatient to reach the end, even though it is still a long time coming, many miles and many more days. To feel the urge to make that extra effort every day is typical, an apparent reaction when so much river is yet out front.

In the headwaters, it was the cold and floods that challenged travelers. But getting close to or past the Chain of Rocks brought heat and sometimes inadequate water levels. Any new trial began as a replacement for one that just ended. My river trip was exhilarating and inspirational during its planning and first paddling. But the thrill could turn after weeks of sleeping out, feeling grimy and wet like a dirty sponge. The thought of finishing sustained enough enthusiasm and suspense to keep paddling despite the abundant, prevailing dangers.

I knew the river trip would be challenging, but I could list only a few reasons before setting off. When they are only thoughts, there are no consequences. Going is still on the mind, like a teenager who has been warned but only scoffs at the caution. They will do whatever they want, regardless, and consult no one. That is real life.

*   *   *

Places outside our comfort can bring hazards, so some prefer sticking to what they know. In Holland, I bought new shoes, then walked my feet to blisters in The Hague because I didn't wait until I was home to wear them. I limped into a pharmacy, saying *Band-Aid* in English, showed my feet and pained face but wobbled out with nothing. I left two puzzled clerks behind. Venturing outside the familiar requires wisdom to survive, which is life on the Mississippi River.

While on the river, I was in flood waters at night, in severe weather without cover, and my boat overturned. I didn't know where to sleep or who I might meet—safety concerns hovered over everything like smog. One time, I experienced excessive dehydration that shrunk me like a raisin, and I missed my family, home, and familiar comforts. This is human weakness, my weakness, but it can arouse vitality and strength to keep going.

In one of my camps, from my riverside, I witnessed a young person stranded on a disabled jet ski. It was too distant to holler, so after an hour of watching them try everything, I called the county sheriff's water patrol and gave our coordinates. Through my scope, I saw the teenager's desperation after unfamiliar circumstances came without warning as the sun slid toward dusk.

Two days before, I felt the same when a river acquaintance met me at a pre-arranged location. We intended to travel on the river together, for a distance and with mutual plans. I had known them for a year and had assisted months before when they were on river miles near my home region. But when they linked up with me, they undid all we had agreed upon for our paddling time together.

Without warning, they ambushed my kayak trip with their self-serving tactics and unbending, disturbing ideas, suddenly invading like a predator. I grasped their noxious intentions after recognizing that their long-term gestures toward friendship were just a lure. They did not want food, my tent or boat, or some gear, nor did they drink all my water, grab my money, or steal my course plots and mapwork. But they followed everything I said with a sentence that began *I want.* This went on for hours, through the overnight, as I sat awake watching and wondering what to do. Their significant wants were constant and considered more compelling than any of mine. It became irritating, unbearable, and very discouraging.

After dozing off for a split second, I woke abruptly with an awareness, as if a message of wisdom had just downloaded to my mind from the empyrean overhead. It was me that the predator was after and without any mercy. I realized it then like a light. They wanted any part of me they could take and would leave the rest in a lump, so I prayed through the night and waited until sunrise.

By morning, I privately decided to go on the river solo as my getaway. I knew I could load up and paddle fast and far all by myself, so as it turned out, I went downriver alone. I used my kayak's rearview mirror to watch as they receded where they stood. Left on the water's edge of Staway Slough, I did not hear of them again. Wisdom. It is like diamonds. We are born without it, so we must never let go when it comes.

Years ago, I left a hotel in Zihuatanejo de Azueta, south of the La Laja River. The outdoor lights were bright enough even after dark. Standing there, I glanced up exactly when a striped owl coasted over me in a slowed motion. It was above the electric lights where the air was a dark night color, mixed deep blue with almost black. But the light below where I was shined upward into the owl's face and underbody. Its wings were held still and outstretched, and its chest pushed down toward me. I saw its face fixed on mine, and its eyes stared into my eyes as it floated on the current so slowly that I thought it was a dream. I knew wisdom was flying over me and dropped some down when I needed it most. So it came to me by the wing this time. The owl appeared full enough to spare some for me and continue on its flight.

Another time in Newton Valley, where nomads walked, some are buried there now, I was driving after midnight. I had come a long way for hours and had sleeping family in the back. The road was winding, and the surface was black like night air, with a drop-off on my side and a rocky wooded wall on the other. I was focused on driving, getting home, and what evil might be with us when I suddenly saw a large white owl drift through the air, motionless, in front of my windshield. The car kept going forward, and the owl continued crossways, neither hitting the other. It turned its head slowly and stared at me as it appeared to hover in place, then disappeared into the dark. I needed wisdom that night also and felt I had received it.

I collected knowledge often and then tried to use it when necessary. This time, it was used immediately to free me and my family from a grip that was not ours. I have learned why humans link owls with wisdom as just a symbol, but for me, it is truth.

The night of the friend-turned-predator was a time when I needed knowledge. There was no owl, so I prayed instead and woke surrounded by spirit. If it was an owl, where was it from? Perhaps it was a supernatural power not easily accessed when awake. Wisdom is pure when it is real. But it matters whose it is – the owl or secret power or given as a gift. I have reached for it often and was freed.

I was physically unharmed by the predator but so sad afterward. Feeling like anyone's prey for hours, I would rather fight off an angry bear. A discouraging mist hung over me as I paddled the river until I eventually found the island camp that was difficult for anyone to see. I stayed two nights to let my spirit reconcile and find its balance. My heart stopped hurting from the human who came as foe after saying, *I am a friend.* A human with no conscience.

I sat on the sand, deep in my thoughts, when I saw the

water patrol arrive to help the stranded teenager. I watched the rescue across the channel and felt relieved as they received help. For me, I wondered how long I would remain out there. Sun, heat, weather, risk, exhaustion, thirst, and a wolf, yet no creature ever encroached or harmed me.

I put up my tent and camping hammock, spread everything out to make myself at home and look like a larger crowd than just me, and then sat in my chair on the sand. I loved this place with all its healing qualities. Hearing animal sounds at night was incredibly restorative, like medicine, when they differed from their quieter day noise or the sound of humans.

A family with children pulled their boat onto a beach across the channel. The distance was so far. They appeared like tiny Legos moving around very small on a vast spread of sand and water. I saw their fire and enjoyed the breezy sounds of voices drifting over to my side in the wind. Just enough to know other people were nearby, but that is often a cold comfort.

I wanted to rise at four in the morning to beat the sun and get on the river by five. That night, I was focused on sleeping with my tent doors open because I wanted to see the monstrous barges slide by in the dark, so close I could almost touch them with my hand. The tug end always came last with a soft rhythmic swoosh and well-tuned shushing at the final distance. I loved hearing it in my sleep. It never went fast but at the same slow plod.

A peaceful rain sprinkled my tent fly, making a perfect sound for rest. But during the previous night, so many barge tows came through that I was frequently awakened or in a continuous half-sleep. I expected the same again the second night. At six mph, the barges used most of this night to get past me and my island. As each turned downstream, the tow's giant headlamp arrived first, toggling, shaky like the river water, and aiming directly at my tent. The light was filled with the shadow of a mayfly swarm as it moved closer. This was surreal, me inside, ripstop nylon between us - the barge, its tow, the insect cloud, rain, the world, and me.

As the barge got closer, mayflies knocked against my tent, hundreds of them sounding like someone throwing tiny mud balls at my house. The beam turned, the light-starved mayflies followed, and the tow silently pushed the barges close to my beach. I unzipped my tent to see them, monster sheets of steel barely moving, and then I worried about mayflies coming in, but they all chased after the tug and abandoned me entirely. The barges were like mammoths silently lumbering, not noticing me as food within reach. It was spooky and awesome, their immense size, movements, energy, and power that later caused the sounds of water slapping on itself as it rolled up on the beach close to my tent.

Afterward, it became quiet until another tow forced itself around the corner. Freight trains ran all night on both sides of the river, alternating their whiney whistles far off. I loved all the noise of machinery combined with the quiet of the water, my island, and its trees.

Last night before bed, I watched the river. It was beyond dusk, but enough of it to make out two forms come silently downriver. One was a few meters ahead of the other and offset a long stream of backwash behind each one. The shapes were identical and enormous, like fluffy medicine balls, and their momentum was steady. The forms glided motionless in a straight line, unlike a water bird's pokey zigzag. They both seemed to float just above the water's surface but must have been on top of it, or they would not have made the wake.

I watched them as they purposefully passed me. We were utterly silent, and neither noticed me on the river's edge. I reached for my scope, but it was too dim. It was not a dream, and I was fully awake as they passed. I questioned what they were then and have wondered about them still. Was it some new kind of wisdom? After all that, I decided to zip up my tent door that night. In daylight, it was easy to make decisions about the dark. But when night came, that was another story.

By the second morning, I had left the island and continued my paddle trip. I stayed close to my things for two days and two nights, hunkered down on a sandy beach with a dark backdrop of trees. I will never forget the small, narrow island as my home. It had no one's interest but mine. Now trapped in my memory as the place I was me, and let it all go. Wisdom had come, valued and brilliant as diamonds.

CHAPTER 19

Roots

Eight in the morning, I pulled my kayak to the edge of the small island beach downriver from Staway's bottomland, many turns below the dam and an old restored fish shack where supper was good. My kayak was loaded after two days and nights of the finest rest in weeks.

This island had all the aspects of Dog Island, but on the river, with pure sand, shade trees, a good breeze, and surrounded by quiet water. It was unoccupied except for me and a flock of pelicans on a small piece of land to the west. My mulishness against leaving was evident when I dug in for the extra day, and certainly in my right to want it.

In pleasant solitude alone, the evanescent nature of living on a river was inspiring and spirit-filled. But it could distress many humans whose taproots go as far-reaching as the roots of a black gum tree. We want our things where we put them, and deep-rootedness keeps them that way. The boat felt more loaded with my stuff than usual, maybe because it held my stubbornness to stay as I prepared for another day in the unknown.

Early this Saturday on the river was quiet, but anticipation for weekend boaters to stir things up was murmuring in my head. I took time breaking down gear and packing, then had water, some protein, and a piece of fruit for breakfast. Despite my reluctance, shoving off the shore of a good camp was a favorite of mine during this river trip. The day was just beginning. My boat was not water-logged yet, the hull was still clean from sand rub, and all things were as comfortable as clean clothes fresh from a basket. The hours ahead were new on the river as if still packaged, unmarred, and high with hope. But, starting out, it is only imagined as flawless.

My morning pack-up and move reminded me of nomadic people groups of the world who lived uprooted but still carried on with others of their own. My thoughts generated a deep wariness, maybe like the feelings of a lost dog who is fine in the moment, but distrustful of what might come. They curl under lonely underbrush at night after the day does not lead them home. Each day's experiences are genuine and realistic for that dog and me, but what has not happened yet and up ahead makes us uneasy. Philopatridomania - an infliction of all living things. Simple, painful homesickness.

*   *   *

Far along on a river trip, each day carried its surprises. Several days previous and many miles ago, I was traveling well, deeply absorbed and reflective. At the same time, I enjoyed the hours of paddling as I moved south and eastward with the river turns. Early came easy with no hazards or complexities, but I noticed riverbanks were mostly unsuitable for a fifteen-foot kayak take-out, and it was nearly past the time for midday food. I saw no breaks on the shore ahead or behind as I went. Water was high and had washed over riverbanks, swept out some fronts, and choked edges already lined with dead trees, now entirely uprooted. What remained had restricted any dry or reliable kayak landing, so I increased my vigilance for a place to hold everything in my favor.

The day wore down, my hunger grew, and nothing came until mealtime was long gone. I stashed a protein bar and apple in the day hatch, so pulling over to access it would be workable but awkward. But I needed a break from the hours sitting with a paddle. The river quickly moved southward as I spotted an island's point up ahead with possibility and smooth ground.

The place was not entirely overgrown, but cut-leaf clusters made the ground surface splotchy, maybe young primrose in the wild but still fresh with early-season green. Even though deserted, this little shoal was filled with signs of previous occupancy, almost otherworldly and not charming or magical in spirit.

Once painted sky-blue, a rusty steel half-drum stood unevenly balanced in the stiff ground after slipping one-sided when floodwater tempered it to mud. Boreholes, drilled willy-nilly above its lower rim to air fire, were filled with hardened ash and riverbank weeds in early spring sizes. Blackened wood chunks scattered on the ground looked like hedgehogs as they crowded the bottom edges of the old barrel. Joe-Pye weed poked up like mint from leftovers of a stone-circled firepit, where small saplings had rooted the perimeter.

A well-tread but narrow trail headed into the skimpy

woods, then split into two as it tracked without clear intention. A weather-worn sign was barely noticeable in a tree with remnants of white painted letters spelling nothing now. Possible remains of a scouting camp, a nighttime fishing stop, or maybe a teenage party spot. Whatever it had been, it was well-used but now forsaken and a secluded reef that filled my needs. Still, I knew I would not overstay. In strange ways, it gave a warm welcome and a lonely desolation, like a wasteland in an end-of-world movie. Maybe it was something done wrong here that turned it.

I slowed my approach before I made the wide U-turn to the bank and lined up starboard. Like dismounting the left of a horse, a kayak's right side is my preferred, but without an apparent reason. A horse's inclination is habitual, as mine might be, or maybe it began as just congenial to my user hand. Once my boat got still along the edge, I sat for a few minutes to further survey the abandoned surroundings and loosen my stiffened bones.

I saw more closely the dirt paths heading into shallow woods like shoestrings rounded whimsically every which way through rooted tree bottoms, made spontaneously and copied over time without efficiency in mind, maybe by noisy playing children and a yowling dog or otherwise creatures seeking the water's edge. Now, it was quiet and thin, easy to peer through the slender trees to a second river channel on the opposite side. More woods were beyond that, all just leafing out for a summer ahead. The thin block of trees, accessible and well-lit, explained the lure of frequent past visitors. But it was now so desolate that a lost dog's homesickness rose in me again.

Despite being early in summer, an old riverbank grapevine

hung in a messy clump from a nearby tree that leaned toward the water. Inside the cluster dangled red and white bobbers and some hooks on wads of knotted fishline. I imagined the remoteness of winter snow here, with bobbers softly clacking and showing off in red against the snowfall, the hooks possibly glistening in the sun. I was reminded of a day on the farm.

*   *   *

I was busy raking soft needles under a bull pine. Each prickle was three inches long, making a fine carpet under the tree. Dry and lengthy, these made perfect fuel for my bee-keeper's smoker. I piled them in five-gallon buckets for hive chores when pine smoke made the bees agreeable, and my hands could poke around inside their brood and nectar. The smoke curled through my hair and clothes, making it worthy of pine tar scent all day, even after the bee work was done. But then, my mind was on the raking and the honeybees waking from winter in the bee yard across the garden, just beyond the chicken house. Some bees were already testing flight outside the hives as the sun warmed the fronts.

Finished with the gathering, I turned toward the adjacent sheep pasture to pick up my pine needle buckets when I saw a Brewer's Blackbird suspended from above, obviously dead from something that happened to it. It was dangling in the air across the fence at my face level. At first, I was astonished and wondered what human hung this bird as a scare or cruel act. But we lived so remote. Who would have done it?

I moved slowly toward the grim sight and saw the bird's neck in a noose of fishline so tight it made an impression in its feather pad. Following the line upward into the branches, I saw it. On a forked bough twelve feet up and surrounded by a shelter of thick pine, a beautiful and well-done nest was securely crotched and woven with a fistful of monofilament all through it. A strand of the line exited the nest and drew downward with the loop that choked the bird when it caught and fell where it died.

Startled, confused, and sad with grief, I knew I was grateful I had not been a witness. But here I am, still giving testimony on the bird's behalf years later. As profound as my emotions went, it was much harder for this bird than for me. I reached for my flip knife and cut it down, then placed it by the roots of their tree.

Back at my mysterious island, hooks and bobbers swaying from fishline off the bunched grapevine were playful and cadenced. It was easy to imagine its music on a wintry, snowy night that would otherwise be silent on the river. But then, a funeral dirge for a wild creature caught in its snag, a helpless mother bird was hanging. High hopes were turned against life for little eggs, baby birds, and the family nest. It's the day that always has the final say.

*　　*　　*

A dry stump sat four feet from the water's edge on this island bank. It was rough-sided with crumbling outer roots, but I could see its old radicle root down its center. If I could catch it with my claw anchor, I would be in business for a secluded and hasty picnic. If something changed or I could not get off here, I would be left tethered to this otherwise handy stump. Cutting the rope and leaving my galvanized claw behind did not appeal to me. But not everything could be a win out here, I reminded myself as I imagined the bird, so I aimed to set the anchor. By the fourth pitch, it hooked without backing out from my hard yank, just as I needed, and my boat was secure.

With my right palm on the weed-stubbled riverbank and the other hand behind at the center of the rear coaming, I steadied my kayak. I had done this dozens of times but only ever on a shore where the keel touched bottom or I could step out with my foot on the riverbed. Here, I could not see through underwater, and my paddle hit nothing when I submerged all eight feet downward. After a couple of tries lifting my weight upward and at once firming the kayak, I went for land. But I missed it.

Only three inches were between the hull and bank after the rope snugged, but it quickly spread as my movement opened a water-filled space. I discovered the anchor line had bunched against a burdock stub at the stump's backside and gathered more slack, a careless detail I missed. With this, the only thing that could happen did. The space between the bank and the boat expanded slowly as my arms spread flat. My body felt the chilly water as it rose against me, my arms forced to widen if my head were to stay above the icy dark river.

I had the urge to laugh aloud but knew better as my day had just changed. My body sank gently into the river like an anchor lowering into the cold from its hawsehole. One arm stretched toward land to hold my weight upward while the other hand gripped tightly to the cockpit as the boat inched outward. Eventually, my fingertips were clinging to the ground and grasping the cockpit bezel, with only me holding things together like a short pulley chain.

Good, the anchoring was helpful. At least my boat did not float away or capsize, but it remained dry and upright. I wondered, while neck-deep and sinking, when my feet would reach the muddy bottom to force an upward push toward air. A well-planned operation had turned, and that new day had a scrape. Ultimately, I toed up the bank and reeled in my kayak. I tightened the anchor rope in a clumsy twist, then used it to draw myself to the dirt, heavily soaked like a flathead catfish.

I finally rested, ate lunch, and dried by the afternoon sun. All this needed and done before a calculated jump into my cockpit to get underway again. Then, goosebumps ran down the back of my neck, as if a breath or soundless puff was made to push me away and gone from there. I was unsure what it was, but I did not look back.

With thoughts of that day well behind me, I paddled the Mississippi River this relaxed morning as I left my island camp of two exceptional nights. I pondered what might become of me on this day I was in. The river surface was glassy and slick, looking easy to slide across in thick socks. It was a morning I loved every time it happened like this. So far, there has been no friction on the water or with my paddle, current, or wind, and no wake from barges or boats.

While at my camp, I watched barge traffic forge straight west before angling this elbow-shaped turn northward into the main channel all night and through the day hours. It was an extra wide bend, sharp as it turned ninety degrees from a ferry crossing. To my advantage, no barges were traveling this perfect morning, or at least not yet. I loved this day as much as the nights I spent listening to barges pass my tent in the dark.

Up ahead, a small boat bobbed close to a sandbar, appearing lopsided from my point of view. I pulled wide as I imagined it abandoned and beginning to go down. The thought and look of a deserted and sinking craft are unsettling, with some persistent unnerving memories. A lost boat belonging to no one, possibly broke loose long ago, began floating silently in night darkness before it stuck itself like a wedge in a river bottom crevice. What eerie spirits inhabited it now after so much solitary floating on its own to places even people have not been?

Years ago, I walked in my farmstead woods and through its soundless ravines on a beautiful day without any trouble. With mind wandering and no disturbances, my eyes lifted suddenly to set on a 1947 Ford Coupe, rusted with torn stringy upholstery and broken springs, planted deep and firm in the side of ravine ground. I do not remember when I first saw this, but it happened several times when I lived there.

With so much missing from the vehicle, the motor, tires, upholstery, cushions, and some controls inside, the steering wheel was still in place. A hard brown surface remained in its original round shape, with fingertip indents formed along its underside and a space where the horn was once placed. In the woods, staring into the car, I wondered whose hands wrapped around that steering wheel and where they might have been traveling. The car had never moved on its own once dumped and likely did not move much by Earth's force or gravity. Its same spot was plain for sixty years or more.

One summer season, my grandchild and friend romped around the car, using it for all types of play. During cold weather, they ran from above and jumped through the wintry air to land in snow mounds on the car roof. By spring season, a red fox and family made a home there with new kits running on the top and through its broken windows. We saw them on mornings in the pasture, sneaking drinks from our pond.

As for the sinking boat up ahead on the river, looking as abandoned as the car, it was not deserted but well-kept and good as new. It was dated a 1959 Lund Baron with an old fisher onboard who I saw as I paddled by. Besides me, only this man was in the quiet cove on his boat, possibly his first and last one ever purchased. As I floated quietly, he looked up and nodded. I waved lightly and kept going. It seemed neither of us wanted to break this remarkably still morning.

After the man, I made my way across the Turkey River confluence and was aware it rises from a ground source one hundred and fifty-three miles to the northwest, just two miles from my birthplace in Howard County. I remember my dad decades earlier standing on the old low-head dam there at the spring-fed lake we still call Vernon Springs. Across the road from it, a walking path disappears along a fence line but ends in a weedy place where stone foundation remnants are still apparent. This was the house of my dad's grandma and my once-great. It was too long ago to recall what happened there, but my aunt says our grandma played cards at her place with a parrot on her shoulder.

I have often thought that Dad would love my river trip if he had been given a whole life. I doubt he'd travel it at his age of ninety-five, but he would observe my journey from home. My vision of him fishing and always outdoors is clear, the same repeatedly and frozen in time. He was the family root cap when he reached his end at twenty-nine, in 1957, in the town near the low dam. This little river, still running from where he fished, pours into the big river several hundred meters from my lost island camp, probably why it rang home to me, as he and I found peace on these waters joined by these two rivers.

After the confluence, I paddled through a small river town, a linear place that runs parallel to the river, protected by levees and without a bridge to cross. Even since their river ferry was built in 1833, the people did not spread to the west bank. One side is all town, and the other is still wild. I continued south and took Picayune Chute to edge around Sweezy to avoid the main channel. A barge moved silently a half mile behind, and I knew I could not manage tow traffic all day.

Picayune was a muddy slough, quiet and calm compared to the channel opposite the island. Along it, I witnessed five bank swallows attacking an eagle without any perceptible let-up. The eagle put up its left wing and then ducked low as they came at it. Then it pressed its wing hard into the air, but they came around to its back and did the same. The eagle pushed one foot at the birds while clutching a large fish in the other, refusing to abandon its food until it was so off-balance that it ran across the rocks to fly off with swallows chasing. I looked at the fish left on the rock and felt sorry the eagle had lost it there.

Two kingfishers were fighting over another fish that one clutched after emerging from the water. The bird looked as if it just stepped out of the shower, head feathers soaked and drippy. The dry one was waiting to swipe the food without working for it. I passed by before that fight was resolved.

It is curious how much conflict humans make together. Then we go to the wild for peace but find the animals are at it, too. Everything is on the move, humans and creatures the

same, hopeful for food, some rest, peace, and comfort wherever we sleep for a night. The birds, that homesick lost dog,
and me.

CHAPTER 20

A Bowl of River

Near the final days of my trip, I paddled an enormous river pool. Remarking to myself how vast it had become, the surface fluctuated and pressed as if someone was holding a large and deep bowl filled with river in the palm of their hand. I felt like a tiny dot, more petite than a cranberry bean floating on top as it rocked. The water made edge-to-edge movements and behaved in a full and powerful way. It did not rise over the bowl edge but went like a giant's packed footsteps, heavy up, then heavy down.

I paddled this entire day, watching sun streaks making shimmery special effects and moving over the top of the lumbering water that was almost groaning from its own load. Of all the miles I skimmed over the Mississippi River, this pool's flair was distinctive. I imagined a bottomless expanse of ground underneath that held up this water intensity and allowed me to ride on top. The cresting green-covered ridges on each side were especially far apart and high-reaching.

I knew it was a dramatic place, pulsating with spirit and energy, never combined like this anywhere I had moved slowly and alone. I felt awe with this swaying motion beneath and the rising earth at the sides. It was a combination of magical, mystical, and supernatural, with vibrations unheard but felt deep inside my blood.

After some hours going southbound here, my down-paddle hit something. It happened before, so I thought nothing of it. Then the other downside hit the same. It wasn't solid like rock but an obvious something. *Maybe fish, large Asian carp,* I wondered. Because I saw nothing, I kept my rhythm. Then both paddle sides hit again back and forth, twice each. I stopped the motion and held the paddle blade down, perpendicular to the water, then plunged as deep as it would go.

This is a usual thing I do to test the depth of my situation and what might be below me – rocks, thick plant life, or something placed there by a human. In this circumstance, my paddle blade went down only as far as its drip ring when it hit something solid but soft. The water texture kept me from seeing it sooner. Strangely, the bottom of this large body of water was only ten inches below my boat and nothing but pure sand. I looked around. Water-topped sand pushed out in each direction as far as my eyes could see, at least as big as our old hayfield and pastures back home.

I continued my paddle work until my kayak jammed to a complete stop on its keel. I was beached like an old, abandoned fishing boat in the center of a monstrous and moving pool of river water only inches deep. I scooted in my kayak seat to move us forward without having to leave my dry cockpit, hoping it would just let go, but nothing.

I hit sandbars before but easily scudded out of the wedge to stay underway. Earlier that day, I had lowered the skeg, so I wondered, *was it jammed deep in the sand bottom like a plow blade?* I yanked on its cord to retract it, but it remained stuck hard. I rose from the cockpit to set foot on this sandy river bottom as cold water filled my kayaking shoes and grabbed at my river pants. Gripping the deck line, I started to walk and pull my loaded boat behind. I hiked half a mile down the middle of a massive river when suddenly, the sandy bottom dropped, instantly gone.

The water hue changed abruptly, from striations of sand and ripples overlaid like laced fingers to the dark smoothness of steel. The startling depth shift caused me to leap back into my kayak and swiftly paddle off. I then saw why I was the lone traveler on this broad, shallow river sweep. The riverbed, unreliable as it rose, then fell away underneath, dropping to oblivion as deep as a whale.

*   *   *

Proven time and again, this river was not to be trusted. If it were human, I could not be its friend. When humans are not really what they put forward, it is complicated to be near them. How is it then with animals? They are generally what we expect just as we see them, consistent in behavior and true in meaning. A bear is frightening all the time, whatever it is doing, even for good reason, until humans tamper to make it dance. Insects are nearly always what we think of them, limited as a primary organism and too simple to show deceit, ego, or some pride.

As a beekeeper, I saw separate individual honeybees while at the hives, but they were so codified in their ways that it was like meeting the same bee over again every visit. They were doing the identical and obvious behaviors I saw before, so they were completely trustworthy. I still love them after many years since I closed up their hives and left. But they fled before me following an unsurvivable cold winter. Like humans, some creatures thieved from these bees, robbing them of order, harmony, and their hard-earned honey, proving that not all bugs are virtuous and innocent.

I came to love and trust a particular animal over the years at my farm. Over two decades, I sat on the porch in summer months and saw a singular and shiny black wasp as if it was dipped in black castor oil. It flew to a tiny slot in the siding near the bottom of the mudroom window. Every season, a singular wasp just like this used the same small opening. Each of the hundreds of times it came, a lime green tree cricket was stunned and held along the cricket hunter's underbelly using its delicate tarsals. The wasp looked like a helicopter as it took the cargo, hovered at the tiny opening, and flew straight in.

During twenty years of observing the same flight and foraging, I didn't remove any siding to see how large the nest or foodstuff had grown. Not wanting to intrude or destroy, I regarded its miniature property as separate from my own. I trusted the wasp and its genetics to gather green crickets, then lay one tiny egg on each as testimony to the hunter's love for precision and ritual. The iridescent wasp was docile as it repetitiously hunted, remained loyal to the old nest behind the shakes of my house, and was never bothered by my presence. Humans are not always as impassioned or reliable as the Cricket Hunter Wasp, and only some can be as true.

The reliable nature of birds bonds me to them and their

ways, too. In a small creaky birdhouse near the kitchen window, a pair of tree sparrows settles and has many babies turn out just like themselves. They lay egg after egg, repeating what they know. We say, *oh look, they are back and at it again,* as if they are our friends returned from winter travel. We only assume these are the same ones that we have come to know and love, who nested early last spring.

Whatever is genuine, visible, and reproducible helps our relationships with any species or behavior. Humans can be unreliable, doing the unexpected, then can be predictable whenever they want. The vacillation is disturbing. There should be room for apprehension around them, like being on a river.

Its sand bottom is shifty like a sea snake, and the mud causes me to sink. The river is feral. That is a fact. Even though people have worked to tame it, they have failed. Its energy has a mind, just like a human, but it is a magnet no less. We cannot stay back from it, like a burning stove, a wild animal, or something opposite to what we know. Even when it is safer to stay home, we go.

We find what is out there and then crave to have it. Wherever eternity is, heavenly and holy, we cannot go and then come back to tell about it like it was our best vacation. I still don't believe some things I've seen, but others I believe but have never seen. Some are unforgettable, yet not everyone has seen such things as a person dying or an infant first breathing, an accident that lasts only seconds, a blackened eye as it rapidly swells, or a streaking meteor that I witnessed in between blinks one morning at sunrise. It streaked, slowly disappearing as if a dream, but lit the sky like a bomb. The river in a bowl and then its vanished bottom, memorable, but I may never see it again in this life.

CHAPTER 21

Six Hundred Fifty · Memory

Months have passed since my river trip on the Mississippi and when I wrote about the last day in my boat. The months since my return are different from life before the trip and during it. I have undergone a dynamic and powerful transformation from being alone on the water, living outdoors, and camping in the wild for many weeks. The changes have positively influenced and developed my spontaneity, mindfulness, contentment, openness, patience, happiness, and inquisitiveness. These are the metamorphic consequences of the river.

I look back to the days I was out there and to the six-hundred-fifty miles I passed over while kayaking. The last days of my trip are now incredibly vivid. I think a lot about them, and as I write, it is nearly palpable as I relive much of it and how it was for me. What good came from doing it, I have wondered many times.

Initially, I did not look directly or precisely at it. What I felt or faced, or the memories that formed around it, were like algae crust on the shell of a turtle over its years in the sea. Clearly, something was there but left unseen.

Some days, a crisp, bright image drops into my view, like flipping on the light in a pitch-black room. Details emerge at that moment as my eyes adjust to the revealed truths of time and experience out there. A scene like this recently appeared as if I had never overlooked it. It was very familiar and a surprise remembrance at the same time.

I was moved from flood waters to a camp below Aitkin's diversion channel. The new site had a level of comfort more elevated than the DNR watercraft camps. I loved the wild camps for paddlers, but this one at Aitkin had extra provisions, a clean hot shower, and a short walk to town for hot food. So I settled in for two nights. When I packed up again to paddle southbound, the river was peaceful and tame, remaining within its banks. I recall thinking, *this is perfect.*

The ride was smooth, and river edges were not far from center. I feel a strong sense of peacefulness and gratitude as I write it. I feel as though I am back there right now. It was so exact and an excellent day as I braided downstream without much wind or interference following the turbulence of flooding, storms, and getting lost upriver.

On this stretch, large homes were set back on groomed lawns pitched slantwise toward the river and flood-proofed. These landowners had the resources to claim their riparian rights with upright docks, stone walls, fresh riprap, and confidence. The landscapes met the wall edges neatly, and the patio or deck space was well-kept with comfy furniture above water level and shielded from rain or wind. I never saw a person but once heard a lawnmower in the distance.

As I went, the riverside properties morphed into fields and dried greens left from last year's overgrowth. I came upon a deteriorating farm, clearly abandoned, with its barn lying flat and the roof on top of the pile, worn like a cap. The old barn-yard was of broken concrete like an overused driveway and near to the riverbank with tall grasses growing up through its cracked slabs. A rusted winch hung in supports with tangled chains that had lifted hay bales or feed buckets to Angus heifers.

The water patrol deputy, who relocated me from flood-water two nights earlier, explained that northern Minnesota did not have season enough to grow bale hay to sustain large herds of cattle. I passed this ghost farm with all signs of former activity, but now it was muted except for the dangling winch chain clinking on itself. Even the wind was quiet, so I won-dered, *is this why the farmer had vanished?* Did they go too big, like the deputy said, in a place that would not have it? No bales and no feed meant no cows until, eventually, no farm. If I hadn't glanced up and scanned the place as I drifted near it, I wouldn't have noticed it was there so proximate to the high riverbank I was passing. Its death was final. The memory of this stretch of river was brought to light for me many months after I returned home.

Residual fear or river sickness did not suppress my thoughts after river travel. But home life had overflowed and spilled into everything, including time and memory. Like wa-ter, it didn't discern where it went. It just went. The minutia poured like this into the freedom of thinking about solitude, harmony, peace, and worry on the river. However, while I was out there, attention was on me only, where I was going, what I was doing, and how things were - right there at any moment. Life is different here at home.

Holding factual evidence of my experiences just below the surface, down in the dermis, it all remains accessible. It gets quietly sifted by all parts of my nature and energy, but it is rarely spoken. This way, I can roll it repeatedly like hard candy turned by the tongue until its center is exposed. Reflecting on it during night hours, bumped against in day, simmered then ignored, the proof lingers. In all ways, it is patiently and privately pondered now that I am home.

*　　*　　*

The day after Aitkin, I paddled dozens of miles slowly and quietly, deep in my spirit, without interruption. I saw only two people up close the entire time, an older man and a woman, curving a bend in an old jon boat, leaving a gentle wake from a trolling motor. They slowed when they saw me, river manners often unseen, and coasted to a stop near my boat as we passed. It was a short, pleasant visit about where we each started and where we were going. Then, have a nice day, and best of luck. This is a good memory.

A second gratifying memory came from further downriver that same day when the land gradually became wooded and brought by open grasses near the banks. A slightly rounded verge lay ahead on the north shore. Large patches of tall, dry grasses began about four feet deep toward an open field, then to a measly arboreous range of leafless growth. Back at the water's edge and the space before the weeds began, I saw movement on a day of rare encounters with living creatures.

So it caught my eye. I did not want to break my slow rhythm by reaching for my scope, so I kept eye contact as I paddled.

The movement on the approach went back and forth, stopping for a second but back again. It stood quiet and watched me while I watched it, then moved again. The river was not wide here, but the water protected us from each other. I was railing the center more toward the way of the opposite bank. The movement showed no signs of wanting to jump in or swim toward me as I got closer.

A canine, nearly the same faded gray-tan color as the dry patches behind it, was pacing quietly as it sized me up. I slowed my paddling and coasted as I likewise sized up the animal. It did not seem precisely domestic or overly excited to see a human. There was no tail wag or body quiver, but some curiosity like a wilder animal might show. I thought this was a young coyote, so I settled on that in my memory of it.

Maybe it was sniffing out some decayed carcass of deer or rabbit or getting ready to chase rodents from the thick grass behind. Coyotes sometimes enjoy a meal of frogs or a lizard, which could explain its nearness to the river that early Sunday. It probably wondered why I was there, too.

I loved that animal and wished the encounter was more synergistic, but I could not pet the ears of a wild one like that, so we were meant to stay apart. I moved downstream on the water, and it sat on land. Its head followed me so slightly I barely noticed its movement. We both enjoyed the distraction but were left unsure. I love remembering it as much as I loved seeing it the first moment. I wanted solitude, but the appearance of this animal and how it looked at me uncovered a lonely feeling that followed me for the rest of my river trip.

CHAPTER 22

Six Hundred Fifty · Fear

While on my river trip, at times, I was afraid. Being frightened does not feel good, but the outcome can be helpful for anyone. People sometimes remain in place while surrounded by boundaries of comfort to avoid feeling fear. What can be squeezed from fear that might be good? What rose from my fear was life. I did not die on the river. I lived.

During mornings on our farm, I crossed the gravel driveway after it came in from the road, turned quickly to the left, and then straight toward the house. At this flex, I saw a mink frog crossing but in a different direction than I was going. I stepped over it and continued to the barn. The following day, another mink frog was in the same spot, so this time, I veered around with my mind on barn things, thinking it must be the same frog as yesterday. When the frog was there again the third morning, I wondered about it more. Was there something nice to eat that brought it here every morning?

For a closer look, I bent down to see it. The mink frog did not hop or move, and its eyes were blank in a forward stare. Its front leg step was halfway up, not touching the ground. After I tapped on its back, it tipped over, dead. I then saw a minor flattened spot on its left hind flank and thigh with some effect on the rear trunk. I knew then that I had brought the truck up the driveway three days ago with a load of feed bags to unload in the pole barn. A truck tire must have nicked its frog body as I rolled by while it minded its own business. We both were minding our business, but it died mid-step in the spot I avoided those mornings on my way to the barn.

This mink frog did not fear leaving home or being away alone but died anyway. It did not survive the outdoors away from the pond reeds below the barn but only appeared as if it was living when I saw it. The frog had been autonomous without fear and concern for home, a confident, experienced adventurist. But it could not endure the freedom of the world that was much too big for it.

The fear I experienced on my river trip did not kill me, like the frog, but it was conquerable as I went six hundred fifty miles in solitude. I was often afraid throughout the journey - of sleeping in mysterious places and doing that alone. I feared what was around each turn of the river or what might be in my trip tomorrow, even when it was not yet happening. I felt fear as I approached each night's camp place, not knowing until I was there whether it would suit me and not knowing until morning if the night would be good for me. Somedays, the weather was my friend. On other days, it turned. This, too, was sometimes frightening.

Uneasiness escorted me each day that I moved toward a

dam and portage or locks. Meeting new people who were helpful to me, all unknowns. I knew I must rise to whatever came, whether suddenly or dragged out all day before I knew how things would go. The good thing is that I survived, and as it turned out, none of it was too much for me to live through, unlike the mink frog. I am better now for doing everything I faced, and still not like any small frog, turtle, or coyote, more defenseless than me in some ways, but still, they all live their entire lives out there. It is impossible to know who will survive what or when our last moment will be.

CHAPTER 23

Six Hundred Fifty · Unable

In many situations on the river, I was unable even though I did what was required to progress and survive. In my ordinary life, I am able, proficient, and competent. I have set my home and community environment within my capabilities. When they are not, I can navigate around or avoid them for as long as I like. Humans can do this with obstacles and challenges beyond the mind of a reptile, amphibian, or any lower mammal. Riding a river with nothing but a small boat, no veering off or avoidant decision is available for everything. A linear trip is like a marble on a track rolling downward, with no turns or jumps for alternatives. That's what it is like on a river.

When I confronted things I felt unable to do, my belief that I might be incapable, more than an actual lack of ability, stirred the fear. At times, I was not artful at all or knowledgeable in the least, so I felt very inept, yet I was able even when I showed a sloppy effort or came near death from trying.

On an afternoon, I paddled into a modest slough, looking for a place to pull for lunch. Afterward, when rested and refreshed, I headed toward the river to continue downstream. A large pad of rootless duckweed coated the surface ahead with no way around, so I decided to glide across it as I paddled toward the channel.

In the past, I have liked the sound of duckweed shushing against my boat as I moved smoothly over it. Usually, it is tranquil but apparent until it is gone. That day, below the expansive surface of duckweed, a field of blunt pondweed monopolized the water, like a bully on a playground hogging all the room. I crossed a short distance before I noticed my hard pull against resistance on my paddle. It felt like a heavy dog adding pointless weight on me or maybe paddling through thick molasses. And my boat and gear, plus me, already weighed nearly two hundred and seventy pounds without this extra. Whatever it was, I could hardly do it.

I worried I was wearing down too soon in the day and was bothered about stamina and ability that I no longer had, even though I had just eaten lunch. What kind of long-distance paddler was I anyway? I agonized as I continued working at the bloodthirsty crossing, much more work than reward. My lunchtime rest and energy were stolen with no apparent purpose or meaning.

How could one quick stop for a meal make the difference between being able and then, unable? I persevered, without choice, in the middle of the large open mire covered in green river vegetation. Below me dangled several feet of thick milfoils that offered refuge to toads and other creatures without concern for my human passage.

Finally arriving at clear water, I glanced back at the length I had traveled. A curving trail left my mark on the solid surface. Then I saw my towline hanging over the stern of my kayak and disappearing like a snake under the water behind. As I reached back to pull it in, I blamed myself for not rolling it better when I used it for tie-up at lunch. But, I found it too weighted to budge.

I yanked on the rope excessively and nearly tipped the boat until its length came above the surface. There, my trouble was revealed. The end hook had dragged through the wide pond of river greens, causing a wad of curly pondweed covered in duckweed to grow to the size of a beachball. I had pulled it underwater over the distance as it collected on itself like a snowball rolling downhill.

It was river debris and not my weakness that had produced the weighted opposition that day. My exertion was necessary. What I called *unable* made me stronger as I worked my muscles against a mysterious challenge. After I untangled the heavy ball and shook it free, I glided more lightly downriver. I felt satisfied that I had that extra strength when a ball of pondweeds caused a needless deadweight drag and a heap of self-doubt.

CHAPTER 24

Six Hundred Fifty ·
Solitary

Throughout the entire trip, I was alone. On rare occasions, I traveled with another paddler, maybe two at once, but they did not take responsibility for me and my belongings, nor did I take care of their affairs. We were pleasant companions for a moment but kept our burdens to ourselves.

Being solitary on the river never left me. It was a strongly felt sense every day. Not good, not bad, just an experience. My life has been spent with very little solitary time because I have lived with my family, and we have been involved in the lives of each other and our friends. My mind has often been preoccupied with each of their comfort and well-being. But fending alone to solve or puzzle through most things is also familiar.

While by myself on the river, new observations were brought to my consciousness. Some people ignored me because they were focused on their reason for being there, like fishing or on their own people while camping and enjoying others. I was an incidental as I paddled through or camped nearby. *If I needed help,* I thought, *would they come for me?* It never happened with random others, but only officials whose job it was, so this was left untested.

I could not find an effective way when caught in flood waters. I saw a man mowing grass at a boat ramp. I paused my kayak to consider whether to wave down a man alone to help a woman alone, me, at a secluded bend in the river. I waited too long because his mower turned in the opposite direction when I finally raised my arms to alert him that I needed help. I was relieved for this. As he moved away, I could not hold my boat motionless for another second. The flood waters were brisk and took me too quickly. I was alone even when I was too slow in signaling for help and missing out on it. Some situations brought out isolation more than others. I was surprised which ones these were but knew I was meant to remain solitary.

I continued paddling a series of switchbacks so full of floodwater it was like a bathtub overfilled and running over its rim. I sensed that a person stepping into it would jostle the edges up and over the riverbank more than it was doing by itself. The straightway before me was wide and flowed rapidly into the leafless tree lines on both sides. It was exhilarating and rattling to paddle alone through this powerful water, so I felt I would welcome companionship.

The next turn showed less than a quarter mile up, but I saw objects on the land just off the overflow at the top of the hairpin. This made me uneasy and more alert, which might have felt different if I were not alone in an inaccessible stretch of this wild river. It was not until I came upon it that I saw what it was - a newly built cabin with all the windows and doors standing open. The interior had been vacated, with cupboards and room doors flung and no living thing moving inside or out. From my position on the river, I could see clear through the cabin, out its rear windows, to the dark forest behind it.

The furnishings were overturned and scattered across the yard, and other belongings were oddly strewn into distant edges of the wooded property. Despite appearing new, it was destroyed. With no people, their signs of trouble were every-where, which felt distressing. A creepy ripple raced through me when I realized its neglect and desolation, like something had gone wrong here and out of control.

I could not stop nor keep going. Neither felt right. But I continued slowly as I passed it, wondering what had hap-pened. This place and its things belonged to someone, but it was isolated now, like me. Some people had started with hope as they imagined playing and resting, leisure with family on the river, but maybe it was ruined by divorce, foreclosure, or death. Some violence got in the way, or someone's returning addiction. It felt like the still silence right after a tragedy.

To the right, on a shallow cove, was a new but unused dock with floating lawn chairs and life vests spilled into the water. It was evidence that something stopped their fun mid-stream or before they ever began. I thought of the mink frog in my driveway and sadly shook my head. Did the flooding do this, or was that after? I was unsure, so I paddled quietly, feeling the acceleration inside me. Whatever happened, it was disastrous for some people. The vacant property had a story but was silent, except for the ghosts I did not want to meet. I picked up my pace and did not look back at it.

Now I am home and sometimes think of the cabin sitting there still, just like I saw it, but in the dark. I imagine an owl, raccoon, some fox, or a night spirit starts to poke at the cast-off stuff. The noise is subtle, but I can hear it like a door lock being tried by someone at night.

I felt strong and most able during these times, even when alone. I liked being with me, apart from others, as a good companion and experience. I could rely on myself while fumbling through amazingly complicated things. I grew to like myself more as I was and the person I had discovered along the way. I will never forget what I faced during those weeks on the river.

CHAPTER 25

Six Hundred Fifty · Unscathed

I was not hurt in any way by others or by accident, but possibly more by my own choices. Exhausted countless times, it was laborious to exit my kayak or climb a high and muddy bank while carrying my gear for night camp after securing my boat or pulling it up top with me. Too tired to cook hot food or read a book, I went without it and often wrote excerpts about the day before a sound sleep.

Now, at home, I have elaborated on these earlier passages to pull them into fuller stories of time spent out there. This was my story of how it went, how I felt, and what was hard for me but maybe not for others. The time I had was different for others who did not do it or for those others who did. All stories are different for each person to hear, and even if the same river, its water is inconsistent and unfamiliar from one paddler to another. Other stories of my times and life encounters are included as they came into my mind every day on my river trip.

I loved doing this river even when it consumed my day's total energy. I became ill, which ended my trip so regrettably and quite suddenly. Neither of these, exhaustion or sickness, was negative for me because, from each, I survived. I rested well at night, never having a scare or danger during sleep except once when I woke with a startle, sat up quickly, and heard my voice whisper, *I hate you*. It did not worry me, nor was it any danger, although I have wondered about it since. It was likely metastasis from another time or a lingering emotion cell or mental virus left behind in a clootie part of my spirit. Maybe the night was filled with dark, floaty particulates that had mistakenly gotten inside. Although, I had visited this very personal tip of an ancient submerged and guarded part of me once before. Still, when I went back to sleep, it evaporated. The experience caused me to feel benevolent toward my new friend. Me.

Besides flooding, fast currents, a near-drowning, a bear that left a scat pile, the human predator, scary weather, deep sinking mud, and the tiny sniffing animal, nothing else came into camp that threatened me or my things, except for one night, a severe storm brought a tornado upriver. I lay hard in my tent, pressing it down when I felt it might rise high in the air. Other than these occasions, it was extra quiet and peace-filled during all other times, and every time very much spirit-filled in my surroundings. In the night, in nature, of water, weather, of my own, during the day, and that of God, filling the air and sky and stars, the sounds and breeze, everything around me I wanted, was so good. Even the thought of a part of me hating another part of me, living dormant somewhere in an old and unseen pointed tine tingling like a tuning fork, it was a truth that was good to unearth. I drenched it with tenderness and a little sorrow for having it.

Otherwise, I woke each morning to the truth, my peace, and a loving sense of who I was with, just me, and where I had rested. I recovered quickly from daily exhaustion and the end illness that brought me home. I knew I was watched over and cared about for my time living on the river and its banks, just as I was kept secure while I have lived here on Earth. Sometimes, it was difficult. And one time, even brutal. But the resilience built within and beyond has strengthened me in ways I could never foresee. I am left unscathed.

CHAPTER 26

Six Hundred
Fifty · Love

I love the river with its temper and moods. I was frightened by the water early but grew to appreciate its boldness and freedom that it does not share with humans. I remember the top water and how it moves at various times on any day—seamlessly going from smooth to rolling and over the kayak bow tip. I love my boat, designed in ways to roll over these waves and push them where they belong. The bow cuts over the water no matter its surface tread and speed. I loved it the whole way down the miles and miles of river.

I love the sand as it appeared from the floods, leaving sludge and fallen trees for hundreds of miles. I loved washing with sand, cleaning the boat hull covered with mud or slime from river water using sand, and hiding my feet from sun while tucked under heavy grains of it. Like memory foam, I love sleeping on sand as it forms my shape, unlike the hard earth or stiff thorny brush.

I have always had a relationship with river features, its water, the banks, personality, sounds, the sand, smells, and even mud. I know the spiritual depth from sleeping next to it, listening to the night sounds of living creatures that sleep all day. Sleeping by sloughs and backwater banks, the night was loud with pleasant and uplifting noise. I loved all parts of this.

I loved the bullfrog after midnight when it called like a soft, gentle tuba, with the same series of notes and then a long pause between. Double-layered notes as if two were doing it, but both sounds came from just one. Over and over, I lay awake to hear it. It kept me up like a late movie. At a far distance, another was the same but smaller in volume. The soft tuba music filled the sluggish stillwater in the wee hours before light. I loved it profoundly and know I will not hear it like this unless I sleep near the water again. It is winter now, but I am already planning my first night back out there for spring.

On the farm, our ponds were filled with boreal choral frogs with three-striped backs, green frogs, and a couple of bullfrogs each. I loved hearing their deafening repetition, but only from the house or barn. It was inevitable that they all stopped singing if I approached quietly on foot. All at once, loud, then a sudden stop when I reached an exact boundary point. They would cease on the same note as if a conductor snapped their stick for immediate silence. I know I must sleep there again so they're unaware and will keep going all night, without that caesura. It was a gratifying experience beyond many others I have ever had. I label it *remarkable, extraordinary,* and *much love.*

* * *

Now, as it is here, the snow is thick and heavy. The air is crackling with bitter cold while I am home during this after-trip time. I cleared much of the snow before it stopped falling at four o'clock in the morning when it was quiet. It is astonishing how thousands of flakes float down to collect on the ground until the snow totals eighteen inches over this winter. On every limb, branch, and twig of hundreds of thousands of bare trees, a layer of fluffy snow has fallen and balanced effortlessly at the same height and depth. Angels must have done this.

I know that individual flakes in perfect shapes give my shovelful its mass. It isn't impossible to understand why some geometers call each of them *sacred* and are impossible for humans to create. As I moved it, I thought about its richness, the life source that makes it fall on us, and so many insignificant snowflakes falling at once without any sound. No big boom or thud is heard as they hit the ground and roofs. If a flake of snow did have its noise, it might go like this: a soft, airy poof. It would be deafening if each of the millions of flakes made this little noise at the exact moment. It is hard to love snow when it is heavy, cold, and wet. But I do.

During this falling and landing and snow-moving, I thought about my river trip and the noise made by frogs at night. I wanted to be back there in the pre-dawn hours, listening to their meetings and discussions in frog language that I could not understand. I know I gained peace from their mumblings.

The snowflakes, so many and so thick, are quiet, with no poofing. The frogs, so few in comparison, were not silent at all. Each of these things is given to us freely from spiritual greatness that we can never measure. For some human reason, though, we still want more. I continue to love all the sounds and commotion out there.

CHAPTER 27

Six Hundred Fifty · Water Paint

I love watercolor paint without any formal training or much experience. Somehow, my deficiencies cause me to love it even more. I enjoy using it to reflect my feelings about the river. Its colors and watery way feel mysterious, nonphysical, and alluring over other mediums like oils or acrylics. I have no gift for doing it or any particular confidence. But it is satisfying and fills me with appreciation, just as it is.

I can stare at watercolor for a long day and never tire of it. The paints and shades, their textures and thickness in appearance, are all beautiful gifts to have near me. I love how we can see through it, but it still has such power. The river is equally these. Textured, powerful, thick, and transparent. I am blessed to love both as I do.

Goodness comes from this paint, but how it goes on paper and is pleasant coming off a brush is mystical. It can run or puddle like river does, but it dries and evaporates into something different from what is laid on so smoothly to absorbent paper. It has its own conduct and will change in ways true to itself, like a river behaving freely.

It is like the night sky in a dark place when so many stars cause a person's breath to wait. When I lived in a vast city for thirty years, its night sky was pink. After a few months, I stopped wondering where the stars had gone. When I spent some time far from the city, where there was little light, I gasped when I saw the dark sky and its millions of stars. It was awesome, a jewel in my memory.

Watercolor paint and the brush are like memory pressed down in thin pieces over a lifetime. They swirl, run, and mix for a human to make a whole, or smooth into the mind like paper recording all one's recollections from decades of living. No one except the painter knows what each brush stroke means when it goes down. Even then, the painter may wonder about it.

As I age, I will sit to think and pray or remember my life, water paint, and time on the river. I might stare at watercolor on paper and not know the difference between it and my memories. Watercolor paint. It is not for everybody but a gift to me. Satisfying and fulfilling, I know what it means and how it reminds me of the river.

CHAPTER 28

Six Hundred Fifty · Done

I traveled on the river less than planned, more than likely. This inexplicable, mysterious, and almost inexpressible kayaking experience will now be with me always. Before launching, a dear friend gave me a page copied from a book. The page was titled *Conquering Your Fears*. She said it might help me on my trip, so I kept it and referred to it while paddling the Mississippi.

Anxiety can grab onto anyone at any time, it read. It may arise from any situation or spiritual attack. Regardless of where it comes from, we must look beyond ourselves when afraid. *Look up,* it said, to get help naming the fear and bringing it to the surface where its aura can be experienced. The paper suggested that exposing the roots of fear may cause it to evaporate.

Like apprehension about darkness, it might be linked to personal history or stories overheard. I asked myself, *why do*

I respond with fear as I do? The page said, *it is how humans face what they fear and can trust when it comes to them this way.* It said, *to face fear by storing the truth in our hearts and knowing that the truth's spirit will protect, help, and support all our breaths and steps.*

I am well after my river trip ended with illness, and I have been at home for many months. Over a multitude of challenges and unknowns, the miles of the river, I am strong, able, and better even than before I did it.

I have love and memory from when I passed over the water for many days. Alone. Just me. I was blessed to have done this and to return home, unlike the mink frog, Millie, my dad, and others who did not return from where they went. The experience and its ending were not intended for all, but for me, this was the plan that happened. I am grateful and fulfilled, and now so much more me because of it.

CHAPTER 29

Writing

I was camped a half mile above river mile six hundred twenty-four on the Upper Mississippi, where I landed in Clayton with plenty of evening in front of me. It was a beautiful day paddling, and made more remarkable when a juvenile bald eagle swept from a riverbank woods without knowing I was there as I floated quietly through. It aimed at a spot in the water about ten yards from my kayak bow, glanced at me quickly as it dropped to the water, and swiped the top with its claws. The eagle soared rapidly with a fish in its feet as if mimicking a diagram how to do it.

Not much later, a smaller pecking bird chased the raptor from its treetop perch after it had pressed the fish to a strong limb with its talons. I wondered if the eagle ate any of its fish meal before being run off by something so small as a Red-winged Blackbird.

During this gorgeous day, I thought about a question brought to me by Sister Karen, who was following my river trip from the beginning. She read the blogs I posted three or four times a week on the *Paddling for Hope* website. Sr. Karen asked about my writing, when I did it, and what I wrote with, while a few others suggested I make a book of it. Of course, that people are interested in what comes from me stirs a good feeling. I very much appreciate being appreciated this way. Questions about this writing have caused me to ask myself the same and take an introspective look at what it is like to write about my life.

I thought I had written like this only once, twenty years ago when I was forty-eight. My grandchild was born, and it became clear I was to raise them. After being together for the first two years, we legalized our bond in court. We became mother and child for always.

During the first months, the baby napped several hours each day. At the same time, I wrote a story about our family, the German ancestors' arrival in the mid-1800s, and how things went after our branch of relatives settled in the Midwest. I included how my thrice great-grandmother, Martha Light, crossed the Mississippi River near La Crosse, in a covered wagon. I wrote about how we spread into northeast Iowa and some of the things that happened to us or because of us. In the end, I had finished eleven chapters that brought me to the baby's birth, and that day I was sitting there writing as they slept. I have tried to understand why I wrote it or how it came from me.

I believed that I had not written anything before this besides academic papers, some letters home, and grocery lists. But since I have been writing about my paddling trip, I have uncovered random paragraphs in files and a few pages stuck inside an old book or journal that I had written about chance thoughts and times throughout my life. I have little memory of writing them, but I recall the subjects as mine.

My most profound times must have pulled the words from places I do not know. When I wrote about family that day, my new young child and I belonged to one another, so I felt our abundance. Now here I am, doing it again, writing about fullness on the river and other places I have been.

I was paddling down a mighty river alone, camping at night in new places, all in the name of hope for humans to change what is in their hearts, again in much solitude. Is it alone time and lots of it that can take a human to unknown cells and molecules inside? Or is it what is outside oneself that does it? The surprise arrival of a baby needing a mom or the depth of water stretched out in front for miles brings hours of wondering about stillness and movement and the fight surrounding me in both infant and river. Deep thinking about how things will turn out is ever-present in both.

Like the baby, I wondered every day what it would be like when I looked back at my river trip many years after knowing its outcome. With a child and the river, there is a certain powerlessness for the end, with little say in how it all will go. Initiating huge things but having only partial effect is like a crumb on a cake, so much responsibility and little authority ever granted.

Introspection came when writing about the river or my grandchild's birth, but also when not writing at all. I have remembered and wondered about moments in lasting detail since my own early life, where many vivid memories took root. Some say I am cursed, or they covet it as a blessing. But as unyielding as this recall is, it has often been both at once.

I meandered along sidewalks, local alleyways, and rural roads surrounding town when I was young. I constantly looked for something but could rarely say what. There I was, poking at things in creek beds, looking beneath and inside the obvious, still watching for that unfound something. I often investigated nearby waterways with my bike fallen in tall grass, shoes tossed, and muddy jeans rolled up.

My youthful and curious wandering was not a search for a longtime hobby or life developed for work. I never knew about bait and reels, which fish line was best, and the specifics of mammal habitats or forest stands. Animals don't even know the name of their species, and I know even less. My seeking wasn't like that, the need to know of science, but more about looking at things out there where they lived. What was I searching for? It was nothing.

How long can a person observe a procession of caterpillars marching or eating off a tender leaf? Grief from an unexplained loss is like this circle of bristly grubs following each other to nowhere. Was it just because they forgot who was leading or because there was no endpoint to the journey? It can be useless and despairing or mesmerizing and rhythmic.

Along the way, we discover many things, alone and together, like the depth of water, our inner light, or darkness in the human mind. Or about truth as a sanctuary, the power of deceit, how peace is pure, and some things about mean hearts. We learn about predators, their prey, our natural weakness and fullness of human strength, and the brave and fainthearted.

All types of complex things walk the earth, whether we like it or not. With hope or without, we are here to stay until we are done. Are we powerless? It does not matter because we make a difference either way. When we trust in something good beyond ourselves, like the sacred, no more is necessary. Living is merely moment after moment, like the caterpillar line. Or more, it is what we say it is. Yet the search is not for the spiritless because it can be exhaustive.

*   *   *

When looking around during childhood, I brought things home for no implied reason at a time when we didn't know to leave them alone. I hooped a metal bucket with a rope handle for things I collected as mine to the old Sears "Free Spirit" bicycle that I shared with my siblings. A baby squirrel caused my mom to screech when I lifted it from the pail, and she saw fleas spread through its fur and over my bare fingers. *Out,* she shouted and pointed hatpin-straight toward the door. After that, I didn't know what happened to the squirrel, abandoned twice that same day by its own mom and then by mine.

Silver Creek flowed from the Upper Iowa River north of town, where I reached it by riding the bike up a gravel road. As the creek drew southwest, I could find its hidden banks below what is now Yankee Avenue, but back then, a north-bound gravel road that ended at the Minnesota line. Near its edges and under the road, I filled the bucket with sand topped with river stones and picked three crawdads from the sandy bottom. Some people used crawdads as bait or supper, but I just wanted them back at home.

It was dinnertime when I arrived and was handed a crinkly, rusted coffee can to hold my animals until morning. I slid the container onto a high second shelf above the junk-covered workbench in our garage, the best dark and cool spot outside the house.

Later that summer, I was upstream of the Kendallville hanging bridge and found a wood turtle in thick river grass. It was a young one, and I wanted to watch it grow at home, so I took it. I had dime store turtles before but knew it would take some convincing to let me keep my stonker, so I kept a low profile for a few days. No one said anything, so I got comfortable with the new turtle.

These wood turtles are intelligent and active, so they are prone to digging around for provisions and curiosity. People say they stomp the ground to rattle earthworms toward the surface, making them think it is raining. But it's common knowledge that a worm has no brain, so it can't think, made only of mouth and bowels. Despite this truth, the wood turtle is much brighter than earthworms and knows how to lure them for supper however they do it.

I love the nature of this turtle species, with a mind of its own and respectable self-reliance when left in its natural habitat, very much like humans. But when tampered with, living things will not reach their potential, whether animal or a person, and will cause them to suffer alone.

The weekend approached when my stepfather said, *let's go to the river with your turtle.* I knew what he meant. They'd seen the turtle, and the answer was no. I went to the garage for red paint and a small brush to mark the turtle's beautiful back. It was smooth with a texture of color only, dull green and buried yellow. At the neck and chin were shapes of brilliant orange that looked like a t-shirt pushing through a collar, then some blotches of orange on the underbody. The wood turtle is beautiful with a pleasant personality.

I painted *Bobbi 547-2768* and *Iowa 1966*, in case someone wanted to know it still belonged to me after we dumped it. I imagined this turtle on its way downstream and to the ocean. But I learned later that they stay close to their hatch point for life if left undisturbed. Suppose this is how it went for this particular wood turtle, that I left it undisturbed. It may have lived to 2006 after I returned it to the water near the footbridge. Raising it from home would have been even better since wood turtles live longer in captivity. Mine could have lived protected at my house until now, 2023, fifty-seven years from the day I found it during my sixth-grade summer.

I also learned that crawdads live a long time alone in a can set on the dark shelf of a garage. After using the red paint from the top shelf for the turtle, I saw my rusty can, forgotten where I had placed it two months before. I ran to the driveway and dumped it on the gravel, a slight panic on my breath. Three yawning crawdads crawled out of the mound of rocky sand, clicking like tapping fingernails on a desk. The sharp sound was unnerving, though I was glad they were alive, so I carried them back to the river on my bike.

*   *   *

Before I saw the eagle as I kayaked upstream from Clayton, I paddled into Billy's Slough for a rest below lock and dam nine. Along Ryan Island near Harper's Ferry, I set my paddle down and tied off for lunch. I was alone and sideways by a tree line and muddy bank where there was no sound. I almost fell asleep while my kayak swayed lightly.

When I opened my eyes, less than three meters from where

I sat, a massive turtle was sitting on mud, like a boulder sunken in deep. At first, I was unsure if it was animal or stone until I noticed a tail and webbed foot with claws. Torn between my curiosity and respect for its privacy, I sat leaning forward, poised to paddle closer, but did not move. It was so large and cumbersome that I knew I could get there before it turned. I measured it with my eyes and believed it had an eighteen-inch diameter and a well-raised back shell. But I sat up in stillness and wondered if anyone had seen this animal before or whether it had ever been touched by a human hand. I speculated if it could be my old wood turtle.

*　　*　　*

Solitude holds silence that is absent when with others. Separation from humans, beyond normal confines, is transcendental. Living creatures of other species know about the super physical otherworld, so often lost to us. The crawdads were imprisoned for weeks in the can, yet they lived and came out singing. It was a mystery then and still now.

Is separateness that mysterious? I crave it anyway, like a bear or tarantula, owls, badgers, bobcats, a single sandpiper making a thin little spink, and the tortoise, these know of it. Think of moles constantly alone and even some insects, such as a praying mantis, separate from a group. Like turtles on a log, they might be among their own, but they come and go solo.

Through writing, I find the diverse and adaptable, separate and together. Cloister me outdoors, away from communal desires, deadly disturbance, or the blurring of self with others. I discover solitude that deepens humans to a place that feels unnatural, but for animals, it is just right as they tend to themselves.

It takes me to write, which I cannot do with others or the noise of voices and sounds, clanking, coming, and going. Writing takes me to it, bringing me back to do more writing. It is spherical, descending, peaceful, odd, focused, absorbed, in-depth, and fun. No velocity or edge is pressing me. Take me deeper and closer, more knowing and wise, every day. Like a snow leopard resting in sun when its hunt is over, this is when answers may come.

Wondering about Sister Karen's questions about writing brought me no answers, but just back to the writing itself. Writing has done many things. It has caused me to connect with people out there when I otherwise indulge in too much solitude. Connecting and separating, like magnets, apart and together, giving and taking, pushing and pulling, from where breathing comes.

Relationships were life-giving on the river as we heard things together, gaining a deep understanding of an experience. My river trip was more than miles paddled or the speed of wind. It was beyond any direction the wind came. The southern wind was worse on the river than a northern, but does it draw us closer or deeper to speak of it? It is about coming alive in more than oneself, more than human elevation, but as high and deep as the nonphysical superhuman lives and waits.

I am grateful for those who followed my trip—reading, commenting, appreciating, and being moved by my writing and encounters on the river, maybe searching alongside me, together and apart. It was an unexplainable experience to connect with others like that. I enjoyed them bringing it to me and living the river with me while I was alone.

Like the child, the river, a hungry bald eagle, or any life of creatures, there is powerlessness and powerfulness toward the end, and control is lost. Yet we keep trying. So I don't have to ask anymore, *for what am I searching,* because I have found it, and it was there all along. It was just me.

CHAPTER 30

Water

Can water be the sister of wind? It is intense and out of our control like the wind, or it can turn to just a trickle for our advantage. Unlike with wind, humans must learn to survive around water because the intuition to hold our breath does not always come naturally, right when needed. Wind does not smother like water, which can steal our breath in moments but refresh and revive in a similar time. When water shifts, it can feel like a backstab, like betrayal from a human we trusted. Water is a single compound but behaves like many, like a shattered mind that makes us uneasy.

It is lovely and calm, clear and tasty in a little sip. But these water drops in quantity can drown living things or rush them away, slamming them against walls and trees. Adding water invites dangerous black mold or wet floors and a dripping roof. But it invigorates a pretty garden or encourages a bath for birds.

My water tales are many. Some are sweet, while others put

my nerves on edge, but all have blindsided me like a stick of lightning ready to strike.

*   *   *

I was undoubtedly not wild as a child, but I said yes to many things as I grew. Twice, I went to distant mountains and stayed so high and deep that the only way down was a rough dirt road of tire furrows. I had no vehicle to ride on those well-worn grooves, so I remained there for weeks.

Nearby, where I stayed, was a cave that drew the interest of three others and me. Inside was a crack in the stone just the right size to slip through toward miles of mysterious rocky tunnels. We crossed a drop-off by pressing our knees against opposite walls and sliding over the narrowed crevasse below. It fell into oblivion and farther than we could ever see.

After this crawl, a second crack was revealed in the darkness, lit only by our clunky Justrite headlamps. This one was smaller than the original entrance, so I was chosen to explore it as the narrowest person back then. I went down on my belly to twist into the hollow on the other side, coiling like a spiral to get in.

The room was so black I could not see my hand at my face and had no idea if there was a cut ahead or another obstacle to my front. I first saw this space when my team passed a lamp through to me. I was in a tiny room, unusually round with sharp creases and wrinkles on the interior surfaces that appeared as close-ups of ancient geomorphologies we ordinarily do not see. Sometimes this is called old-elephant-skin texture and telltale signs of what happened before us. The ceiling was too low to stand, so less than sixty-two inches, and I felt like

I was in a stone bubble. The floor had two parts: the upper where I sat, then a step down to the other.

My light shimmered on the lower floor, and I realized it was an indiscernible pool of water that was clear, smooth, and still. I shouted about it, causing excitement beyond the door as my companions, unable to see in, took my word about its beauty. I thought the miniature pond was a foot deep, its floor mirroring the dry one above.

Reaching my hand through the crystalline surface, I felt the coldness of this untouched and hidden water. I went down into it, my arm covered to the shoulder. Still, I couldn't touch the bottom, no matter how deep I reached. I put in my foot, then my leg, but it was more profound than all this. Like human nature, it had an illusion of shallowness that has been on my mind for years. I still wonder about its depth and whether it ever ended somewhere. Water. It is not of us, and we have no say in how it goes. It is wild and peaceful. It does what it wants, just like its headstrong sibling, wind. I did not know this before that moment. When I think back to the little stone room, I know it is still there fifty years later.

So isolated deep inside a cave system and entered only through a wall crack far in an enormous cavern, its outside opening obscured by jumbled spinneys. It persists dark and quiet still holding its water. I often wonder why I didn't panic in the tight black squeeze. I knew only my approximate coordinates near Bighorn Canyon, and, at that moment, I didn't know how to exit or find road access on my own. Besides, I would still be on foot, and there were no wireless phones in those days.

At my later age, I wouldn't want to enter such a place even

with guides and electric lights. I was free then, not thinking of dangers but of experience instead. Panic in small voids begins with fearfulness, of which I had none. It then progresses to dread the space, as if too small or possibly without an exit. My companions were strangers, yet I was not concerned they would block me inside. Instead, I was awestruck, completely fulfilled because I touched clear-as-crystal unspoiled water and the ancientness of time that day. All the same, many ask me this troubling question anyway, *why did you do that?*

*　　*　　*

On another day in a different year, this one in winter, I found a narrow river where the ice surface was snow-covered and drifting. The snow had blown aside near the edges, revealing cold, hard ice smooth enough to slide on. So, I did this, trying to miss the hard knots frozen to the ice face when I suddenly dropped to the water below. A thin seam broke beneath me, and I slipped right through. The winter wind was cold above, but the ice water below took away my breath. I knew I was in trouble. I don't know how I got out or warmed up again, but the next day in town, a stranger leaned over and said, *I heard you almost drowned.* The water was wild, intense, and dangerous. The first I'd known water so deadly.

*　　*　　*

There was another similar time without the deadly fall into ice water. Instead, it is of me standing by it with frozen memory. I was youthful at the time, home on break, and had asked my mother to drop me at a gravel road south of home. This remote place had rolling hills, deep snow, and frigid winter wind. My memory is only partial, but what I retain is clear, and I was bundled up like a child. Mom questioned me, *are you sure this is what you want* because she could not understand my doing it. I told her yes and got out. Despite her perplexity, she did not stop me but drove back to town.

The place had a large rock formation, and, at the time, it was unkept with overgrowth and left in seclusion. Our local river ordinarily ran through it slow and winding with often-exposed sandbars, crickets, and tiny baby frogs. But not on this snow day.

Years before, my stepfather drove there with the car full of us and buckets with shovels in the trunk. I remember being part of a single-file line, the six of us, as we followed him to a large sandbar concealed in the woods on the opposite bank. This activity was his way of filling our sandboxes back in the yard. This sand was white and soft, worn fine by the river and free because of our labor. It was a good thing he did for us, with us, and many times as we grew up.

Above the river and sand was that jut of the massive rock, outsizing any garage and car but not magnificent to any tourist. A weedy path wiggled up to the top, but on this day, the dry brush was covered with snow as pure white as summer sand. The climb was high but not so much that teenagers held back from leaping off the top into the river below on summer evenings. It was a challenging climb on snowy days like this one, and the drop was onto hardened ice with cold river water flowing further underneath. As a young adult, I stood at the edge of the frozen river that I would paddle years later at its confluence with the Mississippi River. I do not remember returning to town, whether I walked or if my mom came to get me.

Another journey came where I jumped into an ocean swell

at the southwest corner of Mexico, unaware of how deep or feral it was beneath. It was only an instant when I found myself upside down and tossed in loud booming suds, so swift that I didn't even know I had stopped breathing. I have no memory of how long this water had me wrapped in it, but when I got free, I crawled onto the sand, gasping and wondering what became of my sunglasses. This water was so untamed that no one should be in it. Not even me.

But two years later, I buckled up and tied to ropes and sail that floated me high over harsh, turbulent water. People below were waving, so I waved back and then got lost in the silence and breeze high up. When I looked down again, the people were still waving but now yelling and hopping up. I glanced just in time to see I'd rerouted over land. I was squarely traveling toward the roof edge of a beachside bungalow. Immediately, I pulled the right line, twisted it to clear the gable, and descended quickly into the rumbling water. The rescue was swift, and it turned out alright.

*   *   *

All six of my mother's children were sent to water when young, learning to swim and be safe near it from about age five. On summer mornings, we walked barefoot down a squishy tarred road, making imprints on the pitch crust. We'd stop to curl our toes deeper into its surface, and if it left our mark, we knew it was a red-hot day. We hurried along to the cool grass through the park with swimsuits in rolled towels and followed the dirt path as it twisted through shrubs and lilac tunnels. The way widened slightly, then emerged near our local pool.

We learned swim strokes there and to be unafraid. Then,

after lessons, we returned home for lunch and chores. We went back to swimming in the afternoons if our tasks were well done, and we were home by supper. We could swim even more during the evenings if we promised to shower at the pool and get home near bedtime at nine. I was healthy and busy in water for much of my early life.

The pool was closed on rainy days, so I slopped in puddles at the driveway's end. One storm day, I was out there splashing when a man stopped his car and shouted, *you better get in, tornado south of town!* I am unsure whether I went in, but I stood wondering about the southside tornado at the trailer park, envisioning house trailers soaring through the air like many colorful boomerangs. Rain was fun, but I was impatient to get back to swimming.

It was infrequent that I saw my mother at the pool, but without notice, she would sometimes decide to swim. She was on tiptoes, balancing for a dive at the edge of the jumping board. She wore her purple plaid suit with elastic shirring covering its front. Even though I privately thought she looked pretty, no other moms were there swimming when they should have been back at their houses calling us in to eat. Seeing her without more clothes and away from work at home was strange and awkward.

Then, my mom did a subtle bounce before her ruler-straight dive, and her pointed toes entered the water without a splash. No one likely noticed my mom there, just me. I was grown when she died early, and it was much later when I realized she was only thirty-five when embarrassing me at the pool. Because of her, I know about God and how to survive in water.

* * *

It is everything. Water. It kills and saves, gives life, and suffocates. It moves us, then snares us. Mississippi River water is all these things. It is stagnant and rushing, calm but frightening, magical and mundane. I needed water, so thirsty I couldn't douse it this entire day paddling my kayak. Water was everywhere. I was on it, and it was on me. But when floating in a saltwater ocean, thirst can still kill a human. Today, I was on so much water but craved so much more.

I continued paddling downriver from the Turkey River confluence and knew I was running low on drinking water. My concern became more acute with each mile when I thought I saw a pirate ship up ahead and off the right bank. From a distance, I saw a man onboard who was tending to something on deck. As I approached, I noticed his hair and beard were as white as sugar, and his t-shirt read *Pirate's Pit Stop*. He turned and leaned to grab the bow of my kayak and secured it to a cleat on his ship. *I'm Whitey*, he said. A sign ran across the top: *snacks, pop, beer, supplies, gas*. I ordered two cold bottles of pop, hoping to satisfy my thirst, while Whitey sat above me on the deck. He told about all the owners before him and how the snack ship became his.

There were several earlier owners until each retired, Whitey told me. Years prior, Whitey's wife had grown up there so, late in life, they repurchased it to give them work until their own retirement. Together they seemed content on the pirate boat, and everyone who came knew Whitey and his wife - except for me. There were two gas pumps on the pirate deck where boaters filled up for their fun day.

I answered, *yes*, when Whitey offered to fill my water

containers, then watched him walk over a boardwalk away from the ship to land. He took the golf cart in a parking lot to somewhere I could not see. A woman was backing up her food truck to sell cheeseburgers, and a campground was under a rail bridge to the rear. Boaters at Whitey's dock were looking at me and saying, *oh, you're so brave,* and *I'm not as courageous as you!* as I sat waiting for my water bottles. *If it weren't so early, I would stay*, I thought, because I felt more exhausted than courageous. There were campsites, people, cheeseburgers, and the icy water Whitey was bringing.

Instead, I left to paddle down the rest of Picayune to Bunker Chute, where I asked a boat of three anglers why the water was foamy. As if someone flung them from shore, these suds were large clumps with blackened tops and dirty underneath. One angler thought a minute, then said maybe the dam below or the chemicals upriver, not sure, and he didn't seem to care. They said they were there for catfish or any other fish, and the suds did not bother them.

After Bunker Chute, I crossed the channel quickly and went along Hurricane Island's east bank. I could avoid the heavy weekend boating that was on the west and was not up for that traffic anyway. I just believed it was the way to go. I paddled hard without breaking as I watched a cruiser barreling my way without any intention to slow down or avoid a tragedy. I was unsure if they accelerated the double-decker boat when they saw my kayak and me. But the boat was standing nearly plumb as they continued to rapidly approach. I thought about the risk and wondered about humans, then made a run for Hurricane Island by paddling as fast as possible.

The speeding yacht, whose spray foam rose above its over-sized motor, missed me, and the white spume spread too far on each side to be defensive driving. The boater continued increasing speed and raced within meters of my trivial wake, nearly tipping my kayak as their rollers came in. Was it anger, some alcohol, or weak emotion that caused it? Whatever it was, I welcomed the eastern banks of the Hurricane as it eased my situation.

The day was nearly over when I found the dredge island, a sand field a few acres in mass. The surface was pressed with rows of skid tracks from being pushed flat. Green growth was fresh but covered the entire large surface as if planted by a person. The sides were steep, with occasional gentle slopes, and flat sand would be suitable for sleep. I was worn and hungry, especially parched and so tired. As I paddled just below Rosebrook Island, I scanned the dredged sand for a spot to make camp when I saw a perfect place fronted by an enormous lake of still water.

This stump field was created decades earlier when the dam flooded a vast woodland cut low. The stumps still underwater are a hazard to boaters unless a kayaker skims the top like me. The many totipalmate footprints divulged a recent pelican colony that had meandered over the sand here. Otherwise, the sand beach and water were mine for this evening alone.

As I peered around the far edge of the elevated sand, I saw the main channel. It was silent where I was, but I could see cruisers speeding in the distance with telltale white plumes far and west. From this viewpoint, they appeared the size of toys now and ran soundlessly up the channel. I was so hot that I stripped down and took a plunge, then rested in the shade of my tent. Still thirsty and tired, I called home as my heart raced and head pounded. I couldn't get enough water. Something was wrong.

CHAPTER 31

Belong

I woke up early on Sunday after sleeping comfortably atop the sand bank that faced the stump field lake. My tent side faced the river, bright from the morning sun rising over the ridge to the east. The beams hitting the exterior flaps highlighted dash-shaped shadows over the entire surface as if a person silently sprinkled them while I slept. They had worked painstakingly to ensure the forms were widespread and evenly broadcast. The shapes were small, the size of quarter-inch nyjer seeds. I squinted at the top and other three sides of my tent. Nothing there was the same.

The sun streaked hard when I unzipped the tent fly from inside my camp bed. It flashed, so I blinked to see the air filled with fluffy shapes flying in front of my camp and over the early morning still water. It was a cool summer morning, but even now, the little figures looked like light snow drifting upward and around. As I stooped out the zipper door and walked forward into it, I realized it was not just to the front but all across my portion of this sandy island.

When I turned back to see them landing on the nylon tent surface, the settled ones were no longer alive. They looked like lint-shed from a new cotton blanket over a dark sofa, but some people call these white flies in real life, while others claim as woolly aphids. But whatever, every one of the thousands of them was identical in appearance and behavior. They hatched, went aloft, and began dying, all after last night's sunset. Some likely laid eggs, maybe. But whatever details, the flies did it together. One was not discernible from the other. This was programmed into them long ago, and it seemed they had done it since. Creatures do this thing intrinsically. Another way of saying it, *innate*, is built right in from the start.

* * *

I remember paddling in a lagoon during early summer and going along banks and concrete revetments covered with rip-rap to pick off vacated dragonfly nymph casings. One was left gently rocking in my hand while the dragonfly had not yet appeared. It took an hour more to make it out as it shook its form open. Then, it thoughtfully unfolded its wings by trembling insect blood and taking the necessary drawn-out time. This was its exquisite choreography, spreading and nourishing these delicate, refined wings.

My canoe rocked in place with the current while we sat diligently throughout the duration, me, my boat, and the dragonfly. Ultimately, it flew from my palm like it had already been taught to set sail and had somewhere else to be. So untutored but visceral and beautiful in flight.

Always near water, dragonflies dart everywhere, eating tiny

creatures. I have not seen a dragonfly eat, but it is its main activity besides flight. It devours nuisance bugs like mosquitos, gnats, bees, beetles, moths, butterflies, and any flying insect that fits its mouth. It might be said that these things are innate to a dragonfly because it did not have to learn them. I have never seen an elder dragonfly demonstrate flight and speed to a younger one perched on my finger. They know it entirely at once.

Dragonflies consistently reproduce the same. The male finds a female, cleans out sperm left by another, hooks onto her, and flies a while to ensure his genes take hold. He thinks this ensures his sperm is used before a rival comes along. But it is well known that the first sperm is already used even though all dragonfly males perform the cleaning-out ritual confident they are the one. This complete behavior is programmed in, not ever learned. I love to see and understand this, but it does not make sense in the end. Still, it is built into the dragonfly.

Much more complex than bugs and lesser creatures, people still argue about how humans learn. Despite the debate, humans may still need to understand. It may be a little of this or a little of that which makes us who we are or influences how we live out a day. People can learn by watching, listening, or copying. Yet there are some things we do not need to be taught, like breathing, craving food, digesting, startling, weeping, and longing for human connection.

Of course, we are influenced by many things, but one of our most basic emotions at birth is the need to belong. This necessity concerns our emotional imperative to connect with our species, although some relate better with their dogs, cats, or a bird. This may result from a complicated variant to know or share. Humans are more complex than all other living beings.

No matter what the level of complicacy and multi-faceted nature of humans, it is the country of origin, spoken language or dialect, body size, weight, and the texture or color of natural hair or skin that are topics of minor, if any, importance when recognizing that all humans thrive when simply belonging. Inside everyone in our human race is a critical need to be understood and accepted by others of our species.

Contact Theory explains the good in being near one another. No matter who, the connection will then grow and lock right in. A dog can react to our need to cuddle, a cat purrs when we go near, or a bird might like to sit on a shoulder and sing. But it never fills the space inside that linking human-to-human creates. We long for it when we do not have it. We want to preserve it when we do have it. When we had and then lost it, we grieve and yearn for its return. Like air, it's an essential need, yet we are sometimes unaware of its importance or that we often exist without it.

I was fascinated to discover white flies surrounding my campsite and gear. They are naturally sticky and do not just blow away like snowflakes. Even though this gluey feature was annoying, I wanted to know more about them. Insect hatches are remarkable, each day bringing an entirely new population. Typical hatches die in a few hours or a day.

But no matter the white fly enchantment, returning home to our species is essential to humans. And we must never withhold the opportunity to experience the sense of belonging from another human being, if it is in our hands to offer it. If somebody shuns another, they do not fully understand the severity of deprivation they are inflicting unless they have felt it with some insight. Two months ago, I began my solo trip downriver, but today, I packed my kayak and started moving back upstream. My family was coming for me because I was sick, and home is where I belonged.

*   *   *

We were trying a rendezvous at Jim Hollow, where we agreed I could paddle upriver, over and beyond the stump lake. They could find the place guided by GPS and then drive in through an overgrown two-track, broken-down road. In the end, this back lane went underneath the Burlington Northern Santa Fe rails surrounded by overgrowth, and where it dipped so low, the viaduct's underside very nearly grazed the car top. It was remote and isolated, but we hoped to find each other there.

It was still early when I pushed my boat offshore with the white flies stuck to its surface. The water was flat, and no breeze caused any current. As I set off across the enormous expanse of early morning water, I felt surrendered after weeks of pushing and perseverance that tracked my course down all kinds of river terrain.

For the first time, I went slowly with little muscle strength to pull a large or trustworthy stroke. I paddled an hour to reach the far-off bank of the stumps but aimed northeast to make the best use of the crossing. No human was in sight, not even through my spotting scope, but only groups of broody pelicans gathered in shallows too early for a flight.

I have not told anyone this before, but I loved the stump lake and paddling pensively over it. It held beautiful and perfect things at dawn. Water was pure and friendly and all mine, with air still and velvety. No concern for night camp was on me. I would be home soon. Thirst and hunger were unimportant. My people were coming, so we'd eat together like the wilder life around me, quietly minding their business with their own.

I felt like just me, moving slowly over the water like a bird glides in the air, just me with a singular thought. Home. Feeling unwell as I went across, my paddle strokes softer than familiar, my mind wandered back to morning camp.

*   *   *

A rise of sand had pressed flat and firm, creating a crooked ledge stretching along the back of my tent and then for hundreds of feet in each direction around the island's base. It rose a foot in some places, then up to three feet and higher along the way. I had found a fractured cleft just beyond my camp, where I set my press pot of ground coffee and hot water. While it steeped, I sat next to it on the sand rise with my shoulder leaning close toward a loosestrife that I inadvertently touched in some places, and a stem ran up through my hair. I felt weakened and wished I could rest all my weight on its central stalk, and it would push back to keep me up.

It was so quiet where I was. Despite the scrubby bush being criticized and unwanted, I loved sitting there so close to it while neither bothered the other. It had grown to nearly five feet in height and was quite broad. Its spikes of purple reached upward past my head even though I found this place to sit above the ground, where its root base grabbed two feet below me. I heard a soft but strong vibration coming from it. The long spikes covered in exquisite and bright tiny flowers were only made better by the morning sun. There were hundreds of them up and down every stem, so despite their runty size, the plentifulness gave them a grandness I had not expected.

As I counted, twenty-four common Bumble Bees were smoothly working the plant, buzzing and peacefully moving up the spires and across stem by stem. Their energy created silent oscillations that came through the air and struck me like a wind gong. The bees were at peace, they did not quarrel or steal, but their tremolo was coming straight at me from their pureness that was so light, it almost floated. They were not bothered by my closeness, and I had no concern about their proximity to me. I was mesmerized by their morning work, so focused and busy early on my last day. It was apparent they had flown a long way to get to this unsheltered island, just as I had paddled many hundred miles to meet up with them there, at that moment and that spot by this single loosestrife.

The Bumble Bees were cached up with pollen and nectar to make the heavy trip back to their nest, maybe under an overhang of an old fishing shed somewhere or a flooded boat house along the shoreline. I felt eurythmy with the bees, although I was alone on my journey while they were with their species. We were starting that day simultaneously with much silent work ahead for each. Leaving the bees behind woke up melancholy in me that I wondered about. Was it for these bees or for me going off this unknowable and wild river? Some bit of downheartedness comes up in me still now, like leaving a friend without knowing.

I was satisfied with a peaceful trip toward the meeting point. Using coordinates and hope that we would meet at Jim Hollow, I glided along indifferently and wondered if I would ever return here. I could not imagine it while feeling unwell, but my heart was still heavy. I was very heated by now on a cool morning, and my glasses steamed when I exhaled. I wondered what might have changed in me.

I was close to the coordinates two hours in but only saw vast lily fields and thick water plants extending from the banks. Witnessing a break to the landing was impossible, even with a scope, so I sat still in a pool, surveying its edges. Suddenly, I saw rustling from a dense brush less than a quarter mile east. I thought, *bear or deer and fawn, maybe.* Then I saw humans waving and jumping up. There, that was my family.

It was a day more when heatstroke was diagnosed and treatment prescribed. At home, I rested, had good food and water, more rest, and much comfort. I could do this, but as I healed, I wondered if I could return to the river. I heard from a fellow paddler below my last camp who I briefly traveled with upriver. He also had gone home after heatstroke overcame him. He had been hospitalized and then ended his journey. Temperatures downstream had risen to one hundred degrees, with higher in the forecast for the coming week.

I asked my doctor when I could get back on the river, but the answer was *no, not at all.* She said, *you would not overcome again and may not be so blessed.* The paddling for hope ended at six hundred fifty miles and roughly two hundred fifty thousand paddle strokes down this fierce and unruly river. I came home to the familiar, my family, my community, and where I knew I belonged.

*   *   *

Our species needs constant positive and personal interactions with other humans, and we need to know that the bond is assured. When mutual kindness is the bedrock we nurture but only with chosen others – for our family but excluding neighbors, or at work while neglecting the community, at our meeting places but ignoring the schools, in friendships but disregarding acquaintances, or toward one race while ostracizing another - it does not entirely provide so that all can fully flourish. Most know how to contribute, protect, and give, but only to their own.

Like the loosestrife bees or pelican flocks that come together for the common good, these are human functions beyond just the wild and creature world. Broadening skills and beliefs of acceptance outward and toward others could come easy if we wanted to overlook our discomfort. For those we do not know or recognize, who look different, who choose outside our ordinary or show unfamiliar manners or dialect, with those who have different experiences now and before, we still share our same human need to belong. But when close-hearted, it is our very instinct that is slighted.

Paddling on the river for this hope was difficult for me on many days. But all the same, it was my chosen action to recognize our potential for love, open hearts, and the mutual need to belong wherever we live, to come together in a place of home.

CHAPTER 32

Meander

What does this mean to meander? Images imply a winding course, unlike wandering, which goes straight ahead. I have rambled all my life and made up my own definition.

Our sheep flocks appeared to meander as they changed positions while eating across the pastures all day. At nine o'clock, they were at the southeast end of the field, noses to the ground, eating as they walked northward. Minutes later, they made it to the far end of the westside pasture. Not long after, they were nowhere in the open grasses but could be found in the cool shade of the far-off barn.

Sheep constantly travel to forage, many steps daily, but I do not call it meandering. They have a goal, only one thing in mind: food. Sheep are driven by when and what they eat. I have seen a sheep abandon her newborn lamb seconds after it dropped as the mom ewe ran to the barn because she heard the sound of a feed bucket.

Most animals, wild or kept, seek food most of the day, a

clear defense for life. That is not meandering. My meandering is without a goal because the meander itself is the goal and has no concerns or pressure added. It is a state of mind, as meandrous thoughts go from one to the next inside a person's awareness, speaking to another or writing it without a precise shape or plan. A hardened goal motivates but removes that free spirit from the journey. A meander trusts itself to be random, full of potential and experience. Some days, I walk to the store for a small item or two, just enough to be carried home in my pack. This is not a meander. While I might be meandering in my mind, that is not its purpose, but retrieving the food gives it intention. This also takes some spirit out of roaming, which has now become an errand.

My river trip was a meander of heart, mind, and miles. I did not know where I would end each day or what it would be like as I traveled. My mind meandered often, but not if I needed to keep my concentration connected for safety, direction, or provisions.

Writing as storytelling is looping and spiraling, another way to meander. It is filled with ideas that begin and end, then lead to other thoughts. This could go on all day, or at least it does for me. Some people get tired of its endlessness and stop listening. But other stories follow a clear path, not of a meandering style, but with a definite and predetermined end. I am writing about my meandering and early beginnings as I finish my storytelling.

*　　*　　*

I was born in an old brick hospital on the park's east end after midnight on Christmas. Because of this, I have been asked hundreds of times whether I was cheated out of birthday gifts when friends and relatives doubled me up for Christmas. I usually answer *no* because most people have ignored my birthday, instead of doubling up, because they are done thinking of festivities after too much holiday food. Somebody has told me something like this or some other silly reason to miss my birthday every year of my conscious life, but I just roll my eyes. This is the truth about how it has gone, and years have passed since I last pouted about it.

My paternal grandparents were second-generation Americans, and my paternal twice-great grandmother, Martha Light, was Chippewa and born in a covered wagon at a relay station in 1845, just outside Chicago. The city's rapidly growing population had not yet reached five thousand at the time, and many who remained there were born, like Martha, in transit from one place to another. This grandma was born wandering. Three generations back, her family continued to travel until they arrived in Wisconsin, where the crossover at the Mississippi River was straightforward.

Martha married in 1866 when she was twenty-one, then moved fourteen years later to the corner of Iowa that kept our family for generations and bordered the Mississippi River near Minnesota. She spent her life there, keeping house and birthing eleven babies over twenty-three years: Frances, Benjamin, Catherine, Rose, Grace, Nellie, Amelia, Bertha, Maggie, Frankie, and Myrtle – all these my double-great aunts and uncles except Myrtle, who was my great-grandmother.

Myrtle was Martha's youngest daughter, who gave birth to my grandma, Mae, who was then raised by Martha. This made Mae the twelfth baby in line for Martha's nurturing. During all the babies, the wandering stopped, and eventually,

Martha was named the oldest resident in our town of Cresco when she died in 1940 at age ninety-five.

I was born with the meandering spirit thirteen years later. My first solo trip was at age five, a year after my dad had died, and when I packed a sugar sandwich inside a hanky knotted at the end of a stick and took off walking. The adults of my family were preoccupied with their lives, and my mother continued her grief as a widow. So, like most days, I left home unnoticed and enjoyed the nearby woods on second street. Not prone to mischief, I was like my dad, most interested in science and sequence, discovery, and industry of all I came across in the open air.

During numerous summers of my youth, I went door-to-door selling boxed greeting cards to townspeople. Weeks after the work, a large carton arrived, and I'd begin delivering the card boxes to their buyers, all my neighbors, and some family. The best part of this was the premium gift I earned doing my work for the card company. One season, I chose a figure-eight race track with cars that did not function. But, in a better year, I selected a green pup tent as my prize. Before earning it, I was forced to use my uncle's old military tent or clothes-pinned blankets on the line as outdoor shelters because I had nothing else. My new pup tent didn't smell like damp, moldy military canvas or dew-damp blankets of wool. I slept outside so much that I decided to build myself a house out there.

After dragging home oversized boxes from Porter's appliance store one by one, I laced them with shoestrings and other cords to make a cardboard complex. I cut doors from one container to the next to belly-crawl inside my new apartment. I used it many nights until evening dampness or rain downpour moistened it to a soggy, stinking mound. I had to dismantle it for garbage and start over with new cartons. I meandered my town and the fields or woods those nights, exploring and thinking how things progressed to how they were—my years mulling like this developed my way of viewing the world and the things in it.

One summer, I went to Red Owl grocery and placed two cans of Reddi-Wip on the checkout counter. I had the money for it, but the lady looked down at me anyway. *Are you up to mischief, Bobbi?* I answered that I wasn't, which was true, so she let me buy the cans. My plan, implemented with all seriousness, was to walk my usual route east on the gravel to Oak Lawn Cemetery, where my dad was buried. As I went, I held the spray can downward, letting out the spray cream to make a line on the roadbed. My purpose was to see how far it stretched when done like this. It wasn't far, but far enough, I thought.

I have drifted and meandered all my life, nearly all seven decades. I went through Europe and the UK, Mexico, and Canada, and over the states and their cities, especially Chicago, where I finished graduate school and made my adulthood home. I meandered there for over thirty years – walking everywhere day or night, riding the subway, bus, and elevated trains, or biking through alleys and streets to see what was there to see. I ended up in the best neighborhoods and those scariest at times, all so interesting that I went back for more.

In New Orleans, I rode my bicycle through the Garden District when I pulled to a corner to eat my lunch. I enjoyed the day and the relaxation of food while observing the historic surroundings when a woman pulled over in a new fancy car.

She rolled down the window and said, *we don't do that here, so move on!* I think of it now and then, how she claimed the place, its air, and view as if we needed money like hers to see it. I might go back one day to see if things have changed, who is welcome and who is not, and if I can eat on the corner without a scolding.

I was traveling backroads near the Guatemalan border in Mexico when I stopped at a chicken farm. A table was set at the roadside, with chickens pecking around a weedy field behind. I returned as requested in an hour, and a chicken was hot on my plate. It was welcoming and nourishing to come by this countryside home where they let me eat and were willing to give up a chicken for my meal. Although I was vegan, I ate it anyway. I recall strips of wood held up the outdoor sink, and bloody water poured on the ground through an aimless drain hole. It is a place I think about from time to time and wonder if it is still there.

Along a little river, I walked a path through a field. The air was moist and thick while darkness set in, and it smelled fat and full of green plant life. It was dusk, and the sun was gone when I turned toward a road. Any remaining light came from over a low ridge ahead. With careful steps, I walked through the dark toward the dim glow outside a small town.

As I rose over a weed-covered knoll, I lost my breath when I saw a vast field with dark silhouettes of tall grass and broad leaves. Above, for a dozen feet, hovered thousands of Lampyridae with eggs glowing on stalks below. These were thousands of fireflies, glittering and blinking as if hosting a party, not minding my presence or intrusion but warming the air with radiance. The crowd of insects made no sound but lit my way silently to the road back to town.

* * *

My life work was with private clients at my clinical practice on Chicago's northside, where I sat for twenty-five years, day after day, taking in the stories of others. They came for help to untangle or reassemble their experiences and memories because many things are affected over the lifetimes of humans. It was moving through those stories as their minds opened to me that helped me help them. I wonder about some still today, rolling over the hundreds of life accounts I heard in thirty-six thousand hours spent listening. I loved it all. This was another meandering of mine that was enriched by the meandrous lives of those who came.

When I was not doing this at my office, I took my paddling boats out on nearby lagoons, built by the Civilian Conservation Corps with shovels and hands in the 1930s, miles north of Chicago. I spent hours there, too, roaming the lagoon edges in my canoe, looking at what was there. I loved the springtime release of dragonflies from their shells, which I collected and kept for years in small wooden boxes on my desk until they turned to dust.

I paddled northwest in those marshes on a morning to witness a family of ducklings as they were pulled under one by one by snapping turtles, so after that, I named the place Turtle Duck Pond. The adult duck paddled on alone, quacking mournfully after its twelve babies were killed for breakfast.

There was a time I canoed through the great bald cypress swamp on the Pocomoke River in Maryland. The giant swamp spiders and their webs were so enormous that they practically held back my boat as I made my way through the trees and cypress roots, the webs the size of fishing nets. In memory, more than in real life, I am deepened by what I have seen and experienced. I have loved my meandering life, wondering about places and things I have seen, but I always come home.

Countless stories flutter through my mind these days of retirement. People asked, *why do you want to paddle the twenty-four-hundred-mile Mississippi River?* The reason that came to my mind was, *because I can.* But when it was over, it was confirmed that I could not, after all. The river was wild and dangerous, more than anticipated. The weather was hot, worse than ever. After paddling a fourth of it, I returned home.

But the answer comes to me the same, *because I can.* I can. I can try. I am free to attempt it and use whatever fortitude I have been given. I finished a fourth of the river distance but came away with ten times the reward in memory and experience as I learned who I have become. I realize now that the number of miles does not compare with the depth and scope of a person's life.

That is the freedom of my life, and I hope for everyone. We can meander for the effort, not the ending goal, and be unafraid, all humans. I want to explore worlds I have not touched or have never touched me, see people from other places, eat food not tasted, and be interested in all the many things out there. The details of the world stack up in my mind and make rich thoughts for later. The earth is more than what we see or think we know. It is deeper, more microscopic, more profound, and inward, more magnificent than any one day. It is not electronics, a movie screen, or showing it all at once.

The world, its pieces, and nature are magnificent and dimensional, dynamic beyond any dream or imagination as it keeps moving or remains sitting still. Like the river, it has a mind of its own and is made by another, not by us, but for us. Its supernatural power rights itself when off-balance, heals when harmed, and grows again, time after time after time. It never loses its roundedness.

Paddling for Hope, at last, represents that it belongs to us. We all should have it. Not me, not you, but us, until no one is afraid to go out and see the world. However old or young, whatever color or culture, we are the same. No matter what we were born, who we are, or where we live, we are all given Earth. It is composed for us. The extravagance of what is holy excites the call for us to be free. Its immensity is not beyond every human grasp. Meander.

CHAPTER 33

Almost

Walking to where I am now, I felt the sun's heat pierce the tree shade along a nearby road. It was not solid blotches of shade but thinly dispersed and unreliable, keeping it too hot for a late autumn day. In these same moments, a cool wind was whirling through. I felt the heat and cool unmixed as if opening the freezer compartment in a hot kitchen. The apparent cold did not break the heat but kept a fine line between them. This is how things go, no wider than the edge of a thread separating two things while maintaining their difference. It is what happens, warm and cool, light to shade, life or death.

We traveled a far distance one night, and the whole family saw a set of headlights shift lanes into ours and come straight at us without hesitation. As it rapidly came closer, we all started to shriek. The oncoming car never took its lane back but kept at us. We could not move against the shoulder guard at our edge, so we were jammed. The advancing driver was passing someone, so all three vehicles were in jeopardy. Suddenly, the side guard ended and provided a momentary pull-off. Our gran knew what she was doing when she hoicked our car into the unexpected opening. It saved everyone. I could hear Gran whisper her prayer of thanks.

This is an extraordinary apposition of it-did-happen, then it-did-not-happen. The story is not the same the next day when you say you were *almost* killed. People nod and go on with their own day's business. But another second, a trace this way or a fraction further another way, the story would be different, and everyone would tell it all the next day. Some people would feel entitled to be the one with information and more brutal details, turning our misfortune into small-town gossip. But good, it only *almost* happened.

During my trip on the river, I confronted polarities that were challenges but not tragedies, hazardous yet fortunately not deadly. The stories were alarming, though still endurable. A tornado tore through but did not lift me or move my things to other places. Flooding was fast and frantic, but I slept soundly on high, dry ground at night. After being sucked into deep and thick mud, I washed off and emerged to tell of it after the Coast Guard came to my rescue.

Some days before, my near-drowning was only *almost*, so no one cried at my funeral. The water had threatened but did not take my life as I hung inverted below its surface. I was conscious and wondering if this was it for me. Then I imagined breathing in this thick, spoiled water waiting at my face instead of the cool, clear air I saw above. A single second stood between me and permanent darkness, but it was no big deal since I did not actually drown, but just *almost*.

My river trip did not *almost* end, but it did end when I came home with a common illness, not death or an uncourageous spirit. It was a recoverable condition, although it might not have finished like that a day later. I admit to having a bit of confusion and a racing heart, a pounding headache, and so dry from dehydration that I thought I was in the Atacama Desert, no matter how much water I devoured or heard splashing around me. Heat raged inside me while the outside air was over ninety degrees Fahrenheit, yet as I clung to my shrinking lion's heart, the river did not beat me, but only *almost*.

Humans go all the way, I know I do, with all types of rites and passages or dares to reach further, and we mostly continue to exist while telling the story of it, even if it gets too dull and no one wants to hear it. That is because it is usually just *almost*. To overcome, that is solid as rock. Nothing is frivolous about prevailing over fear or trauma, addiction, the unknown, poverty, and homelessness, or being chased through the dark as pounding feet get closer. *Almost* robbed of a self or made to feel nothing, a future gone, knuckling down, torn apart to separate loved ones, breaking but not yet defeated, not even a little bit. This is a testimony, mine, or it could be yours.

Almost drowned countless times, *almost* dying in a nighttime smashup, manipulated by those with no good in their heart. I have never seen a hurricane or tornado, but I could have. Then, I might have *almost* died as it swirled nearer and much faster. Though I know it was very close to me.

I *almost* fell from a high mountain ledge in Appalachia but did not. I saw how far down as I leaped across a gap, but I was younger and thought I could fly if necessary. We can fly, free, not by our own power but in the air over everything natural, nothing unique except borrowed power.

Years ago, I hitchhiked across the country without foresight who would come for me. A semi-truck took me over three states, and its driver was kind. A family with no home but living in an old Chevy station wagon let me jam into the rear. When we reached a concrete median three hundred miles later, I jumped out to rush across several lanes to catch a bus on a bridge.

It was not for nothing but for something: surviving, getting there, moving, seeing, remembering, and going out again. This never ends, not even *almost*. It is here and now, then gone. That is how it goes for all of us on Earth. Never sure, but still going, learning, trying, and wanting more.

*   *   *

When an extra-long cold and brutal winter was predicted, I *almost* gave up sheep farming. Seventy-eight bred sheep were in our two barns, and the prospect of feeding them twice daily for six months was overwhelming. It wasn't the work of it but the management and amounts of grain, alfalfa, and thawed water necessary for the extra-long winter that challenged my fortitude. I read that feeding winter barley grass would increase nutrition and lambing numbers, but I had no idea how to grow it in our upper midwest winter.

Almost a magic bullet, barley is rich in fiber, many minerals, and vitamins and high in thiamine, protein, vitamin B complex, niacin, manganese, and phosphorus. Learning that barley was especially good for fetal growth, ewe health, hydration, food craving reduction, and conversion of winter feed persuaded me, but I still did not know how to provide it to the animals. After much research and talking with Brian, a family member growing it for horses, I *almost* felt I could try it.

I emptied a spare room next to our farmhouse kitchen, and my family helped me load two-by-fours through an open window. I constructed a ceiling-high, wall-to-wall frame with four angled slots where I placed four full sheets of pink insulation board, four by eight feet each. They slid in and out of the slots like tilted drawers. Each sheet was divided with a plastic strip, so in the end, I had eight equal sections in which I poured a thick layer of barley seed, one segment each day over a week. Our enclosed front porch held pallets with a thousand pounds of barley seed waiting in burlap sacks.

Above my homemade rack, I copied Brian's plans and rigged a PVC pipe drilled with holes across its length and a timed garden hose attached to one end. Water was sprinkled from the tube onto the top sheet every few hours, trickled slowly under the barley seed layer, and poured onto the staggered sheets below. The freshwater cascaded until it splashed into a tilted gutter at the lowest sheet and flowed through a tube into the basement drain.

Each tray sequentially grew six inches of fresh barley grass, a thick pad of hulls, and a three-inch layer of white roots. This took seven days each, so I labeled the trays: Sunday, Monday, Tuesday, Wednesday, Thursday, Friday, Saturday, and Extra Snack on the eighth tray. We cut each fifty-pound pad into small squares and delivered them to the sheep every morning by tossing them over the fence into the snow-covered barnyards.

The sheep ate better in blizzards that year than in any

springtime. I love the memory of our white sheep in snow-white winter with bright green grasses protruding from their lips. If sheep can look happy, ours did. That year was a lot of winter work, and I *almost* abandoned the barley project, but our pregnant ewes gave twin and triplet lambs over eight weeks of spring, March to May.

This story is about adventure, like hitchhiking or jumping a gulley, riding a river, and swimming in an ocean rise. It was daring, widening and deepening, exciting, and new – for all of us, the sheep, my family, and me. I shudder when I imagine that I *almost* did not build it, *almost* lost my nerve, *almost* did not grow barley in my house, and *almost* missed the pleasure of lambs in doubles and triples. The memory is satisfying and intricate with detail. I loved the aroma of fresh-grown barley in January and could smell it like a garden while I slept. It was warm as it grew and wet enough to quench a cold sheep's thirst. But to think, I *almost* made me miss it.

I am completely alive, not just *almost*. My journey is crammed with memories from life before and now life after this river. I want to tell of it and share about those whose lives crossed mine, both the people and the many things. Now I am here, home, and trying to write this book. Not to *almost* write it or make an *almost* book, but to really do it. To rightly hold and read and have it, and to want it and give it. To set it on a shelf and, years later, find it topped with dust.

Actual, genuine, and not *almost*. This is my victory over, pushing further than any previous dream, exploration, or thought to do something I ought not or that I have not yet done, or I have gone and done it anyway. Push out the sides that pulse at the narrow edge to go further, if only just that one unused step. I challenge me, and I challenge you. Reach beyond where we cannot see, for something that matters, whether for you or someone. The motivation is truth and acceptance that memories do sustain and hope does restore.

WHY I PADDLED FOR HOPE

I grew up in rural Iowa in the fifties and sixties. When I left my home region for college and career, I saw people different from what I saw at home. The dormitories were evenly split among a variety of people groups. I lived among Asian, Middle Eastern, Hispanic, and Black women on the residential floors of the college. Not long after, I attended graduate school in downtown Chicago, where fewer students were white compared to the rest of the resident population. My first long-term job was at a Black-majority city college with a substantial BIPOC student and faculty population.

After years of acclimating into a world much broader and different from my rural upbringing, visiting my still mostly-white community was challenging. The mindset of a culture accustomed to a white majority can become hackneyed when it remains comfortable in homogenous customs, beliefs, and experiences.

During the 1960s in northeast Iowa, two significant events occurred concerning race that deeply affected me. Because growing up in an undiversified culture does not stir momentum and interest to seek out differences, I was surprised that both happened where I lived during my formative years.

The first event was at the local swimming pool. It was integral to our small-town tradition to spend the summer at the pool, first learning to swim and then swimming during most afternoons and evenings. There was not much else to do, plus we enjoyed it. Everyone knew everybody else, wore similar swimming suits, each had one old towel, and abided by the same customs, generation after generation. Sameness was the norm.

However, for at least two summers of my memory, a bus transporting Black children pulled into the swimming pool parking lot. If I remember correctly, this happened more than one day, maybe for two full weeks, when children of color joined us in our pool. I was inquisitive and excited but do not remember conflict after our commingling. I do not recall white swimmers leaving the pool while the Black children swam. I remember watching our visitors play with us, jumping in from the diving line, standing on deck, and using the water floats. I was very fascinated by their black skin. I knew I liked them and enjoyed their visit. We were different from one another, and they were from Minneapolis. No one told me anything. It is just all that I surmised on my own.

I was not privy to how it happened, but being among people different from my community and me was fun and exhilarating. I don't know how other families and townspeople felt or reacted, but my family was welcoming. Someone in town planned, approved, and implemented the visits more than once, bringing the children from two hours away. It is an exceptional, fond, and first memory of contact with people different from me.

*　　*　　*

The second thing happened in a town that sat on the same state highway as my small town but twenty-three miles directly west. Something remarkable occurred in Riceville, population 898 at the time, and undoubtedly all-white. Not only was an Olympic athlete born there, and two U.S. Foreign Service Ambassadors were raised in Riceville, but a third-grade teacher at the local school challenged racism and prejudice the day after Martin Luther King Jr. was assassinated.

Jane Elliott was a thirty-three-year-old Riceville native from a large farm family and a graduate of the Riceville school district's all-white student body. She also was an anti-racist who is now a famous diversity educator at eighty-nine years old.

It was 1968 in her small Iowa town when Elliott conducted an exercise with her third-grade students called *Blue Eyes/Brown Eyes*. Children were separated into two groups: the blue-eyed and the brown-eyed. Each day, one eye-colored group was singled out and treated as inferior. The students in the ostracized group received less recess time, were ignored, and were treated poorly. Other anti-discrimination teachings were inserted into the lessons as Elliott taught what became an infamous curriculum.

The *Blue Eye/Brown Eye* experiment has been featured on PBS, The Tonight Show, at a White House conference, as an ABC documentary, the subject of two books, five times on the Oprah Winfrey Show, and the college-level documentary titled *The Angry Eye*. The students who were part of the original teaching returned as adults to tell how the project positively affected their lives. Some have shared how angry they felt when part of the marginalized eye-color group. But still today, the grown children of Elliott's class experiment express gratitude for learning about discrimination in this poignant manner. They have described how the anti-racist lessons influenced the raising of their own children.

In 2009, a version of Elliott's exercise was broadcast on *Channel 4*, Britain's public television, entitled *The Event: How Racist Are You?* Jane Elliott received *The Hillman Prize*, an award associated with social justice and progressive public policy, among other awards and citations. Stepping out as she did caused a disturbance in her small town and for her family, who was ostracized and called racist slurs.

My mother was a teacher in a nearby elementary school around this same time and shared Jane Elliott's stories with me. She applied some of the lessons in her classroom about dignity, fairness, and mutuality. I thank my mom for this as a gift she gave me. Its basis is love, not hate. It is the way to an open heart. I love peace among people while together and different, acceptance of others, all in the same breath at once, who are not the same as me, and an openness to learn from other ways and cultures.

Three decades passed when I moved to a small farm from the city. So near La Crosse, it was where my family and I visited and did farm errands for twenty years. I was conscious of the low number of people of color and the slow growth of integrating neighbors over the years.

In the early 2020s, I sold my family farm to retire in a La Crosse neighborhood and finally called it my home. Without intention, La Crosse has figured into my early, middle, and now retired life. For decades, I witnessed its drowsy movement toward wholeheartedly accepting people's differences in the community. In late 2020, I saw the film *Amplifying the Voices of Black Youth and Their Parents in the La Crosse Area* when I was the leader of the Serve Team for Justice at a local church. Little did I know what would result from viewing this film.

It was the stories I heard and the people who told them. Their pain and its depth were palpable and cutting. I felt immediate affection and respect and wanted to know them personally. Their expressed struggles were right there, where I lived, and caused by people who treated me well and who I identify with and rely upon. My people. I was embarrassed, hurt, and angry after hearing these stories. Whether mean-hearted, ignorant, or untaught, it did not matter to me. The roots are unconscionable traces of a heart problem within the dominating culture and its people.

The film's voices told stories of marginalization, insult, and degradation, denial of housing or suitable living conditions, insufficient and unmannerly customer service in some local businesses, racial disparity in schools, and second-rate provision at some nonprofit agencies where everyone is entitled to the same. There have been stories of race-based refusal to assist Black families the same as white home buyers when attempting to purchase homes or move ahead. It became clear how deeply race is an issue. Citywide, there was a lack of role modeling and economic stimulus through race-based hiring practices in professional and working-class positions. Then I realized it: I rarely encountered a person of color or ethnic difference in public or at any appointment, whether medical, financial, or when shopping. My heart was broken, and I didn't know what to do.

I contacted people who were instrumental in making and distributing the film. I asked if they could locate some participants and see if they would allow me to speak with them. After two months, I received communication that we could talk over Zoom.

The day of the scheduled meeting was monumental. It was my first meeting with Shy and Mya, directors at a local community center that serves our Black neighbors in La Crosse. Ten minutes into our Zoom, Shy said we should meet in person. After I asked when, she said *now!* I drove over, and we met in person for the first time.

Not long after, I was introduced to Mia and Chaya, both officers of the Black Student Leaders, and other student members in the film. Over three years, I have been honored to work with these community leaders on educational, housing, and other life-building issues.

In 2021, I had a personal idea to paddle the Mississippi River after reading about the Source-to-Sea River Trip. It was on my mind often as I planned and assessed if I should attempt it. During the months of research and preparation, I felt a barrenness that should not accompany such a fantastic adventure, but it felt empty, almost like sleep without dreaming. Eventually, I realized that my solitary kayak journey lacked meaningful collaboration with others.

I decided to add a fundraiser or an awareness-building event to my paddle trip. Without experience or knowledge in this area, I reached out to others I thought could pair my journey with an effort to raise awareness for diversity. I felt a fundamental need to focus on a more mutual, unified, diverse community. If human hearts can change to feel more love toward our neighbors of difference, we can change our choices, experiences, and lives in our city to be even better.

My effort to find help for the undertaking was unsuccessful. The individuals I spoke with did not have the time or experience to take it on. Knowing I could not do both the paddling and the initiative, I told Shy I was sorry that I had to forgo a fundraising and awareness campaign, because I could not find anyone to lead it. But Shy said that she would do it. And she did.

My paddle trip and the local event joined other community organizations, individuals, local media, city services, and the mayor's office to spread the message. The *Paddling for Hope* initiative became real as it flooded across America and the globe, reaching ten countries beyond our own. People worldwide joined on social media, our *Paddling for Hope* website, and through donations and events to raise awareness for equality. *Paddling for Hope* was accomplished with over 13000 Facebook page visits, 2100 website visits, nearly 7000 web sessions, 9000 blog views, six hundred fifty miles paddled, and thirty thousand dollars donated. A launch party, paddle-through gathering, and media attention were organized.

During the summer of *Paddling for Hope*, change did happen, and hope was fulfilled. It had happened since my first vision of racial difference and disparity in 1968 when I was in eighth grade, and Reverend Martin Luther King Jr. was assassinated. Movement forward and hope gave us this chance. Sixty years ago, Dr. King spoke:

"Five score years ago, a great American, in whose symbolic shadow we stand today, signed the Emancipation Proclamation. This momentous decree came as a great beacon light of

Hope to millions of Negro slaves who had been seared in the flames of withering injustice. It came as a joyous daybreak to end the long night of their captivity. But 100 years later, the Negro still is not free. One hundred years later, the life of the Negro is still sadly crippled by the manacles of segregation and the chains of discrimination. One hundred years later, the Negro lives on a lonely island of poverty in the midst of a vast ocean of material prosperity. One hundred years later the Negro is still languished in the corners of American society and finds himself in exile in his own land. And so we've come here today to dramatize a shameful condition."

In our city today, we must continue to change how we think, how we see, what we do, and what we do not do, how we speak, and the words we say. There is no other way to bring us into a cohesive community beyond just one kind, but all people, all together. Everyone must be regarded with respect and dignity, all backgrounds, all experiences, all history, and all dreams going forward. Differences bring curiosity and vibrancy to our community. We are the same in ways that can hold us together, bring out empathy and compassion, and nourish an equal and mutual sense of belonging.

Only humans endorse this note of separation, one from another, groups over others, some diminished and excluded. This is fabricated by people, not from another world, nor celestial by energy or spirit, from nothing around us, or anything above us. We make it up and then authorize it, ignoring that it causes suffering. A people crowd of all ways, colors, sizes, and races, speaking every language ever created, will gather. It is a crowd larger than we have seen, inclusive and dignified, not demanding. Everyone is the same, facing the same, feeling the same, and knowing. There is only one way and victory, which is not ours. There is only one God, and I am not it. This is the truth on water. It hurts me when a human, any person, or community feels unloved, dishonored, trivial, and disgraced. This is why I paddled for hope.

ACKNOWLEDGEMENTS

My river trip and book writing were accomplished with the love and support of others. I thank those who were with me in body, mind, prayer, or spirit. My family who never rested until I came home. My friends who did not try to stop me. All those who reached out, commented, thought of me, asked questions, answered mine, and offered support of all kinds. Those on the planning and creative team who did faceless tasks and mundane jobs that made things work. Those who supported Paddling for Hope, near and far, in any way they could. Those who knew me a long time ago but reconnected because my trip was meaningful to them. Those who went on the river before I did, paving a way, sending knowledge, experience, and empowerment downstream to me. Those who offered to host me on the river when they did not have to open their homes. Those who coordinated my book completion, and who read, proofed, edited, commented, and guided my book writing. Those who brought me food, drove for miles, rescued me, and brought me home. Those of various sheriff department water patrol and first responders who aid paddlers in need, like me. Those who worried the entire time I was gone and who had a friend named Freddie years ago, and who I love no matter what. Those who died too soon but would have been near me if they were still on Earth. To my dog who waited at the door until I came home. Most of all, God. To all of those and everyone, thank you from deep in my heart. My gratitude and love always.

www.ingramcontent.com/pod-product-compliance
Lightning Source LLC
Chambersburg PA
CBHW030404130626
46549CB00004B/1629